DORSET DIARIES

For friends, known and unknown, who may have read these pieces in Country Life.

DORSET DIARIES
A Dog's Life and other Jottings

DAVID EDELSTEN

HALSGROVE

First published in 2004 by Halsgrove
Text © 2004 David Edelsten

ISBN 1 84114 401 0

British Library Cataloguing-in-Publication-Data
A CIP data record for this book is available from the British Library

HALSGROVE
Halsgrove House
Lower Moor Way
Tiverton EX16 6SS
Tel: 01884 243242
Fax: 01884 243325
E-mail: sales@halsgrove.com
Website: www.halsgrove.com

Printed and bound in Great Britain by
CPI Bath

FOREWORD

David Edelsten and I are neighbours – he Dorset, I Wiltshire. Though in separate counties, we do not live far apart. Our surroundings are, however, as so often in the West of England, quite different. His are hills, hedges and small fields; mine the longer vistas at the western edge of Salisbury Plain. Our houses differ also. Mine is a typical village manor-house, no intentional shape and no discernible style or period. David's is, as I thought the first time I saw it, perfection of old rectories, late-Georgian, beautifully proportioned and fitted out inside with cabinet-makers woodwork.

I knew David before I knew his house. We first met 40 years ago in the Officer's Mess at Sandhurst where I was a junior member of the academic staff, he a recently-joined captain instructor. I took to him at once, partly because of his elegance – he was wearing the tailored battledress of the 13th/18th Royal Hussars – partly because I identified him at once as that distinctive military type, the bookish officer. He liked horses, as every hussar should, but he was also well-read and wanted to be a writer – which, as we know, he has become.

David is also a hunting man, which I am not because, being disabled, I cannot mount a horse. At the moment, moreover, he is a disgruntled hunting man because of the Bill outlawing hunting, currently passing through Parliament. I do not altogether share his feelings about the ban because, having never hunted, I do not know the sensations of following hounds that he describes so eloquently. I do, however, endorse his principles. My view is that since foxes have to be culled, let people hunt them on horseback if that is what they choose to do.

The government is alienating rural constituencies from another direction with its plan to reorganise the regimental system. Many of those connected with hunting are also connected, as is David Edelsten, with our historic regiments. His charged at Balaclava with the Light Brigade.

The powers that be are foolish if they think they can tinker forever with the fixed points in our way of life. The county hunts and the county regiments represent historic elements of our national system, with which a government concerned to assure its future tampers at its peril. David Edelsten, writing from Glanvilles Wootton, does so as a deep-rooted West

Countryman. He represents both an historic Western institution, the South Dorset Hunt, and historic ingredients of our country's military history, the 13th and the 18th Hussars, today the Light Dragoons. His father and my father-in-law were country doctors, with neighbouring practices straddling the Dorset–Somerset border. Deeply respected servants of their local communities they are remembered to this day, 30 years after their deaths. The sort of families they founded, to which David and I belong, brought up to contribute to the county and to maintain values and standards, hear never a word of thanks for their efforts, let alone thanks for what we pay in taxes to support our fellow citizens. Least of all do we hear words of apology for the attack so-called progressive politicians make on the institutions we hold dear.

Officialdom, on which David makes frequent and well-judged attacks, dislikes the use of the name of 'England'. Officialdom perhaps remembers G.K. Chesterton's refrain 'We are people of England and we have not spoken yet'. May David Edelsten's voice long be heard.

John Keegan

INTRODUCTION
On being allowed to sing...

To answer a question I am often asked, the opportunity to write came quite by chance – but it was a chance that I was ready for.

Having arrived at the end of my school-days without the least sense of a vocation, I am very much in sympathy with aimless youth. The great thing was to do *something*. 'Why not join a cavalry regiment?' my perceptive House Tutor at Clifton asked, so I followed my passion for riding horses and enlisted: the Army was mother and brother to me for over 30 years. I don't think that there is anything quite like a British regiment for what I can only describe as all-round, old-fashioned virtues in a world gone mad.

At Sandhurst came another signpost. One of the old schoolmasters on the teaching staff beckoned me aside – 'You have a way with words, cherish it!' he said. I did. Wherever the Army took me, my father posted me bundles of paperbacks, which I read, and read, and read. My *beau idéal* was Edith Somerville, author of *The Irish RM*, I adored her epigrammatic style and self-deprecating humour, and tried consciously to mimic it.

The pull of home eventually took me out of the Army to a job at Taunton, running a charity that aimed to help the drunks and druggies of Somerset. A couple of years into that the telephone rang, it was my eldest stepdaughter – a regular diarist had dropped out, could I fill a page in *Country Life*... can a duck swim!?

Apart from the first article (which appeared in *Country Life* in June 2000), these are all diary pieces that I wrote from and about this household and this village over the next 13 years. I am very grateful to the Editor for his permission to reprint them.

D.E.
The Old Rectory
Glanvilles Wootton
July 2004

THIS IS HOME

You would be hard put to it to say exactly where the heart of our village lies, or to name its special talent, but we who live here think of ourselves as being among God's elect. You would certainly go bankrupt if you tried to sell picture postcards of the place; it is a nondescript scatter of mostly modern dwellings. There is little but our name, and a rustic gem of a church, to remind us of our Norman predecessors, and only the earthworks on Dungeon Hill above us to remind them that they were Johnny-come-lately incomers.

The church stands to one side of the village, in the fields almost. Some say that the villagers moved their houses from an adjacent meadow after the Black Death. The field is called Stonylongs, which, since there are no stones in it to speak of, suggests it might have been a source of building stone in later centuries. But we don't know – there is very little that we do know about our village's history, we just know that we are fortunate to live here.

Perhaps its situation is its special charm. We are on the floor of the great Vale of Blackmore, which Thomas Hardy called the 'Vale of Little Diaries'; not lost in its middle though, but snug up against its wainscot, the Dorset Heights. Every day, half a dozen times or more, I look south to the line of the ancient Ridgeway, a thoroughfare since prehistoric times. That skyline means home to me; I have carried its picture in my head the world over. Now that I am finally settled here, I ride up to our horizon, or onto Dungeon, two or three times a week, look down below me, and bless my good luck in belonging to such a spot as Glanvilles Wootton.

Ours is a farming village. When we came here 50 years ago there were 13 herds milked in this small parish, and 13 lots of churns to be trundled to the roadside for collection daily: now there are just five herds on the modern tanker's round. But still the business of the place is farming, turning the rich vale grass into human food; still the farming clock sounds the primes and vespers of our day; and still the farming calendar dictates the rhythm of our year.

If there is one time in that year which more than any other characterises us, it must be the evening of our Harvest Festival. Then the church is full to bursting, and – as I imagine, since I have never seen it – it must seem from outside like a jewelled, tuneful, lantern hanging in the fields. We all have supper together afterwards, church and chapel, in the Village Hall, and my friend the rector, who was an auctioneer before he got the calling, sells all the produce from the church, to much friendly banter, rivalry and merriment.

There is a funny thing about that Village Hall. Empty, it is a draughty, unlovely, soulless place, but we never leave after an evening there, my wife and I, not having enjoyed ourselves. It is at occasions in the hall that the village contemplates itself, everyone mucks in, and, if one must use a word begrimed with bureaucratic fingerprints, we feel we are a community.

We are an old-fashioned lot, not much impressed by urban notions of modernity. The great issues that nightly furrow the brows of television news presenters, and are presumed to rack the nation, often pass us by. Indeed, the 'forces of conservatism' run deep in Glanvilles Wootton: we expect nothing but foolishness from government or London, nor yet from Dorchester or Blandford, and seldom are we disappointed.

I do not know what the Saxons hereabouts may have thought of the incoming Normans all those years ago, but we have been lucky with our incomers in more recent times. Perhaps it is because they have come singly, or in ones and twos, and they have come, not to colonise but to belong to us, and have had the sense to listen to the music, before attempting to join in the dance.

Like the game of Cluedo, we have our stock characters. It is a truth uni-versally acknowledged, that every rural village needs its Colonel Mustard, its retired senior officer... and that it is a dire misfortune to have two. Our Brigadier is indispensable and quite harmless. He keeps us all on time, makes sure chairmen of committees do not ramble, reads the lesson in church audibly, and, of course, from the King James Bible, and, when he is not exercising his horse, or hunting, or being walked out by his beloved lurcher, is often to be seen tending the war memorial, or sweeping the church path. On Remembrance Sunday he clanks about in an array of peacetime medals, and at the annual fête he minds the gate.

The Brigadier is an incomer of course, he came here as a schoolboy shortly after the Second World War, and, although he must be nearly 70, many still think of him as just the doctor's son. His contribution is what he would call 'good order and military discipline'; others have come since, bringing wealth, worldly wisdom and employment, all badly needed.

Some of us, notably my 91-year-old mother, exclaim at the changes in our village. It is true that, in this past generation, we have lost both of our two pubs, our forge, and worst of all, our school – a shrewd blow that, by the siege-engines of crass modernity. But, myself, I find it a near miracle how little the essential character of this beloved place has altered.

Was it really five years ago that we buried old George Dunning? It seems like yesterday. But I have the evidence of his funeral service sheet beside me: his 88 years all but filled the twentieth century. 'Will ye vollow on pleaze?' the usher asked, leading me to an unfamiliar pew – we have our own language still, much as William Barnes recorded it.

The church was overflowing, full almost completely with farmers and their wives, the eulogy given by the grandsire of our strongest local farming dynasty. He had gone through school with George, and swapped best-man duties with him. We sang the favourite farming hymns, and finished with 'The day thou gavest, Lord, is ended', words almost unbearable in that context, before leaving George in our beautiful churchyard.

I have just been to visit George's grave. I had forgotten that Nellie, five years his senior, born almost with the late century, had left him full 14 years a widower. They lie together just a few paces from a corner of a flint-stone chapel built by Sybilla de Glanville in the reign of Edward III, among the 'rude Forefathers of the hamlet'.

Is this lovely place perhaps the heart of our village? Like my namesake the psalmist, I lifted my eyes to the hills, to that reassuring ridgeline, and thought: 'This is England, this is Dorset, this is home.'

JUNE

Mares are notoriously shy about foaling. Daisy, a matronly Irish hunter, at what we assume was her first attempt, seemed no more likely than most to observe sociable hours, but she surprised us all. At about supper time on Saturday, before being brought in for the night, she started pawing the ground, lying down and getting up again, and generally indicating that her time had come. She was a fortnight overdue, but mares all round here have been holding on, seemingly for warmer weather.

It was all over in an hour, but not before her fan club had gathered. Daisy's pregnancy had been a matter of note and frequent enquiry locally. Alert eyes across the lane had seen what we had seen, and the whole village, or so it seemed, turned out to witness what must be one of the rarest of countryside sights.

With really no problem she produced a fine, large colt foal. Another hour saw him on his feet to a muted cheer from behind the hedge, where a debate had started as to what he should be called. By the time he was being carried to the privacy of the stable, it was a settled thing that Daisy's colt was to be Dandelion. His birth and naming had been public events, and were duly announced in church the following morning for the benefit of the few who had not been there.

Perdita seemed the right name for the small lurcher, or large whippet, who mysteriously joined us last summer. She just turned up in a neighbour's garage, naked, exhausted and famished, lay down and refused to budge. It is an out-of-the-way spot. How she got there or where she same from no one can tell.

She did not have an easy fostering. Lovable and winning though she is, she was wild out of doors and barbaric in the house. To her, working surfaces were walking surfaces. Confidence among local chickens slumped. It was touch and go but, despite many an anxious debate and the odd propitiatory fiver, she survived, and she has thrived.

Exercise was always a problem: she obviously needed lots of it. The breakthrough came when we discovered that she could be safely led off a horse. In fact, she loves it, has become biddable and almost totally obedient. The sight of a hard hat or a riding whip is enough to have her hanging round the stable door, popping on and off the mounting block.

The only worry is deer: at the flash of a distant scut she forgets everything. On Easter Day, in some frantic and illicit pursuit, she unzipped her bosom on barbed wire. The assembled family said: 'That wound must be stitched.' The vet said 'Let it heal itself (that will be £30 please).' It did.

Over a game of bridge the other night, a kind friend told us that one should not let whippets run flat out before they are two years old: it harms their hearts. If that is true, it's too late for Perdie's heart, and I know she has damaged mine. If I was ever to have a dog, it had to be a whippet: that had been settled long ago. Perdita's guardian angel and mine must have put their heads together.

SEPTEMBER

Evidently we are in for an embarrassment of apples again. It happens every year, although we do nothing to deserve it. About one winter in three I rush out, and, in a Sergeant Troy-like frenzy of flashing steel, reduce the overweening trees to due subservience. But they get no sprays, nor do we have any of those greaseproof garters that you see, or used to see, on demure trunks in better-regulated orchards hereabouts.

Most of our trees are very old indeed. Their limbs zigzag in all directions, picturesquely recording the more rational pruning of responsible generations long past, when the apple crop really mattered. My unscientific efforts produce, year in, year out, sacks full of apples for our neighbours, who probably do not want them but are too polite to say so, buckets full for the stables, where their welcome is beyond doubt, boxes for the house, which will keep us supplied until next spring, and rotting barrow loads for the compost heap. It is like the loaves and fishes.

Over the orchard wall lies the graveyard. The parson of the day built our wall on his own land leaving a narrow, useless strip this side of the bedraggled remnant of a hedge – a no-man's-land where the detritus of years of burials and pious visiting has been dumped. When I came to clear this noisome purlieu some time back, it was no pleasant surprise to find thigh-bones and bits of skull among the plastic flowers and knobs of clay. Sextons must grow thick skins if they work in country churchyards, where grave encroaches on unremembered grave. I dumped the lot in a dry pond, now levelled; a fitter resting place and no less hallowed. The hedge is levelled also, the land consecrated and in use. A friend's ashes lie there; I mean to lie there too.

Meanwhile I live in hope that one of our four children will wed a vet and settle locally. My wife is extremely tender-hearted about our animals and all their bodily ills. The slightest, muffled cough from the stables sets her in a spin, the state of the sheep's bowels causes sleepless nights, and Perdita's childish ailments bring life to a halt. Horace Hayes[1] is seldom in his due place on my shelves if I should want him, and taking temperatures, a squalid, anxious business, is a frequent chore, not helped by the fact that none of us seems to know exactly what is normal for all our patients.

I love our vet, but I do not love receiving his bills. We must be much of an age, he and I. When he first came to these parts he was a young man and on his promotion; I admired him then, and I admire him now. When we show him a horse that is lame or sick I know that he has seen a hundred like it. His word is gospel to us, and he has become a power in the land. Yet I doubt his A levels, or whatever, were up to much. Would he pass into veterinary school now? Would Nelson pass fit into the Royal Navy?

A white stocking is a good practical point in a dark-coloured horse. I miss Daisy's stocking, she that foaled last April, when I quarter the five acres of Chantry Mead early on a hunting morning looking for Woody, Venus or The Bean, who have not a white leg between them. (Semi-retired, Daisy is staying with friends in Somerset.) When I find them, then comes a moment that repays all the sweat and labour, all the heartbreak of owning horses, and the vet's bills. Woody blows half a snort, puts his muzzle to me and seems to say, 'Is it you old fellow, all right...?'

DECEMBER

Down here in the vale drainage can be an obsession: most of the few squabbles I have known in the village have been about surface water, ditches, or the general working or abuse of a system designed so skilfully by our forefathers. In December, as the water-table rises and gateway mud deepens, we really appreciate their ancient labours.

It stands to reason that the first thing done when this parsonage got

---

[1] *Veterinary Notes for Horse Owners* by Captain Horace Hayes – a classic.

its Georgian front, was the laying of the cellar drain. From a floor grid it flowed (or should have) I knew not where, until four summers back when the outflow was uncovered. A mere 50yds away, when our northern boundary ditch was cleared, 8ft down, the digger found a stone drain which flowed. The cellar is rarely dry in winter, but the water is much lower now: before the outlet was freed I sometimes could not get dry-foot to the wine bins, even in gumboots. Now, the level seldom covers the bottom step. 'Why not install a pump?' I am often asked. I have no answer. But our house is not unduly damp, and perhaps it would go rather hard with the frogs and efts who make their home down there.

Just as St Patrick banished snakes from Ireland, so Perdita has sent our kitchen slugs packing. It was clear from the earliest days that, like a fox, she relished slugs, so it is no surprise that her domain should be a no-go area for them. But, once she had decided, and we had conceded, that the cosiest room in the house was to be her sleeping quarters, we soon forgot that a hazard of coming bleary-eyed to the kitchen in the small hours had been to encounter a great, slimy, orange battleship, tirelessly navigating the tiled floor, or that the panelled back of the window seat where I sit at breakfast used to be criss-crossed with silvery trails each morning. Yet, when Perdie slept in the stable during her first heat, the slugs were back at once, battleships, trails and all.

But here's the mystery. Perdie never seems to stir at night. I can't be sure, but I feel certain that she does not quit her bean-bag from last hug to first wag. She is glued there in enviable, child-like slumber, from 10 till about 8. She even ignores my early comings and goings. So, do the slugs know she is there and not venture out? How come there are no short, zap-ended trails on floor or panelling? I must suppose that slugs can smell and reason and have the wit to bide their time, although I never would have guessed it.

Venus is the unlikely name of the family cob, a chubby, gypsy type, part Welsh. I well remember how we first learnt what she was called as she stood in all her roly-poly plenitude in the dealer's yard: it was difficult to keep a straight face then, and I smile now to think of it. But she has a lovely head – it is a case of 'Nice face, shame about the legs'. We bought her five years ago to replace my wife's first schoolmaster, and she bridged a gap. But she has not the scope to go with safety in the demanding vale country hereabouts.

All of us ride Venus at a push, but not in the vale. She is loaned and bor-rowed, and has a dozen lovers. She adores hunting and goes anywhere on the downland, away from the big fly-fences.

Venus has faults, who hasn't? She's cloth-footed and will stumble if you let her and, since moon-blindness injured the vision in one eye, is not entirely steady with overtaking traffic. But in the summer when I go and talk to her at grass, and she puts her forehead on my chest, and rubs her poor, fly-pestered eyes and face on me so trustingly, I worship her a little.

JANUARY

Nothing looks more dishevelled, hung-over and woebegone than a hunter the morning after a long day in a muddy country like ours. There were two such to deal with after breakfast on New Year's Day.

There is no end to argument about how horses should be treated after hunting. Those who believe in immediate hosing-down, elaborate bandaging or late-night brushing will not be reconciled to those of us who follow the 'leave them alone, and brush tomorrow' practice.

What we are all worried about, however, is mud fever, which takes root under warm, moist, mud-sealed hair and, once started, is difficult to cure. It is, moreover, painful to the horse, disfiguring and, in the heel, can lead to lameness.

Another aspect of managing horses after heavy work which all agree on is the need to have them warm, dry and snug before the jockey settles for the night. Again, how this is done is a source of schism. Our system (which is, of course, the only right one) is to turn the horses out to grass for a brief romp in a small paddock by the stables immediately on returning home, almost however late, and in almost any weather. That way they have a chance to roll, to line their bellies with a bite of grass and to commune with each other.

This seems to unwind them, to cool down their bodies and their psyches: at least, we have found it the surest way of preventing 'breaking out', the late-night sweats of an excited horse, which can make settling for the night so difficult for mount and man.

Our church stands in the fields, apart from the village, the centre of a star of ancient paths and bridle-ways. It is pleasant to picture past congregations gathering on foot from outlying farms and hamlets, dressed for the occasion of the week, and then dispersing to the week's best meal.

At least I hope it was so, for we all know that the rustic idyll is a myth. For certain, in living memory, the people from the great house that used to stand on Dungeon walked over the fields to matins. The other evening, as light failed, I was glad to turn Woody off the road and take the bridle-path which crosses a field called Stonylongs for church and home: I could just descry the outlines of buildings and familiar trees, when some cautious person, perhaps with that primitive fear of graveyards most of us acknowledge, following a wobbly torch, entered and lighted up the nave.

Riding and leading on the morning of our first hard frost this tardy winter, I was more than usually appreciative of the courtesy of drivers on our byroads. It is a different story on the main road, especially in summer, but on our back ways it is rare to meet a driver who does not allow for the unpredictability of a frightened horse. I always try to show my gratitude, but with both hands full, this can be difficult.

Truck drivers are particularly kind, none more so than my friend with the milk tanker. There used to be a school bus in this area with broad black and yellow stripes all across its cab, the equivalent in nature of the terrorist's balaclava. When Daisy, who is a touch neurotic, was suddenly confronted by this elephant-sized hornet, she spun round and bolted. I was lucky to go with her, and we both were lucky that she kept her feet and that the road was clear behind us.

The other thing Daisy could not face was a giant concrete mixer, churning on the move. What she thought that was I cannot guess, but she always took exception to it, and I really cannot blame her.

MARCH

If you look south from here, a mile or so away the downland comes to a sudden halt, forming a memorable skyline. Memorable to me at least, for, wherever I have been in the world, the silhouettes of Dogbury and High Stoy have gone with me as the epitome of home.

Travellers from earlier days have used those heights to dodge the hazards of the vale – mud and, in lawless times, far worse than mud. Tess used that route on a late-December morning, the frosty ground 'ringing under her feet like an anvil'. I used it one recent Saturday when it was too cold to hunt, riding and leading, following the same way, thinking of her.

The track runs on over Dogbury, crossing today's main road at the Devil's Kitchen, and skirts the side of High Stoy, following a north-facing contour. What was once a significant route is only a byroad now. Picking its neglected way across the tide of modern traffic, it goes from nowhere special to nowhere of importance, via paradise. For this sheltered place, called Remedy, a vernacular piece of Dorset woodland, is the most lovely spot on earth for me.

All sorts of native trees, some exotic ones, and every kind of under-growth, flourish here. Often in cloud, it is seldom dry. Old oaks carry armfuls of fern and moss, and hart's tongue is everywhere. Squirrels, scampering in the vaulted branches overhead, send down showers of accumulated moisture on us as we pass. The wood has a ruin, an old loading bay I guess, or it might have been a kiln, beside a long-disused pit or quarry. One can picture the carters, their charges biding their time there, perhaps enjoying a nosebag, while the laborious task of loading was in hand.

As you leave the wood, and start descending to the vale, a path I know well heads off left up the hill, guarded at its entrance by a leaning oak which seems to threaten those who pass that way. It is a tree that Arthur Rackham might have drawn. I fancy that I see the receding figure of poor, fated Tess go up there as I head the other way for home. She went on to an encounter at the Cross in Hand, a strange wayside stone on the hilltop, which was to lead in time to Winchester gaol and to the gallows. Her path, after a seductive start, runs almost like a flue, straight up the hill, and is a scree of flintstones underfoot. A single horse can manage it, but I would not ride and lead that way. We took the safe, slow-descending road.

The end of March means, shortly after, the end of another hunting season. Woody and I have been out with hounds nearly 40 times since our first day cubbing in September. They were not full days, no horse could stand that, but they were good half days or more, and at least half a dozen times we stayed until the hounds went home. Woody is a remarkably sound horse.

A local bobby said to a friend of ours recently, 'You must need to be thick-skinned to go hunting nowadays': a remark that is at once outra-geous and quite true. It is difficult to think of an activity that is more politically incorrect than foxhunting. Why do we do it?

All of us who hunt find, I suspect, different pleasures in it. For me, to have the freedom of familiar country, to try to read the actions of the hounds and keep in touch with them, to gallop and to jump a trusted horse, and to bring him safely home, spell deep contentment.

MAY

I often question whether nor not a life seemingly devoted to the wants and welfare, not to mention to the hygiene, of domesticated animals can be entirely sane. The reader can perhaps form an opinion if I describe a recent, not untypical weekend.

Teatime, Friday, home from work, and Wimp was in labour. Not near the house, of course, but in the farthest corner of the five acres of Chantry Mead. If 'Wimp' seems a misnomer for the biggest, woolliest, white-faced sheep you ever saw, I ask you to believe that the name once accurately described her. She was, as I remember, thrown in for nothing with a batch of orphan lambs we bought six years ago. Looking then like a small fragment of a chewed pipe-cleaner, her chances of survival seemed worthless.

Yet she throve, has usually borne triplets, unassisted, and has been a perfect mother to them. She has been almost a trouble-free sheep: we love her, and she loves us, whom she still thinks to be her parents. She usually calls to us, and comes to be petted when the occasion offers.

Lambs normally arrive on time, and Wimp was one day short of the full term of 147, but she seemed to be troubled. The reason soon appeared. One, and only one, very large, as I thought, ram lamb painfully emerged with a little help. Wimp and her babe soon started that exchange of unique bleats and contented rumbles that will become the call-signs of their foolproof homing system.

On Saturday, three out of five horses were to be galloped, grazed, groomed and generally got ready for team chasing on the morrow. Perdie, who has become a deer-addict, would need separate exercise, and our flock of six ewes had to be brought closer to the house. It was a full agenda.

You would not thank me for an account of the morning routine of a household centred on stabled horses. Suffice it to say that the necessity of early feeding, and of the delightfully misnamed chore of 'skipping out' (removing night-soil from the horses' beds before they trample it), precedes a peaceful breakfast. Then plans can be made and tasks allotted. It fell to me to take Venus, the family cob and spare tyre, for her workout, and to my wife to take the edge off Perdita's exuberance. We then would ride the big horses out together.

Venus done and put out to grass, I set out with the expander to ring Wimp's lamb. All who keep animals suffer the necessity of inflicting pain on them. I hate ringing, placing a ligature on unwanted appendages. If properly done, and early, it does not hurt the lamb. But there is the risk of hurt, and I have never yet reduced the operation to a butterflies-free routine. So, plodding out reluctantly, the gadget and a supply of rings in my pocket, I longed to be done with it. You may judge my pleasure when, on turning up the little mite, I found myself looking at a female undercarriage. Ewe lambs need names and this one was easy. She had three regularly spaced black spots on a diagonal across her tiny flank, for all the world like a die; she had to be Dotty.

As I left Wimp, I saw that Blackie, the matron of our flock, had started labour. There was just time to gallop the second string before returning to obstetrics. By rights, lambs should arrive as wedge-shaped bundles, two little hoofs and a nose leading the dive for life. But all too often they present themselves like tangled washing, needing a midwife to extract them. There was no way that Blackie's lambs could emerge unaided – all three were malpresented, with legs to be manoeuvred forward. My wife, with her small hands, is the consultant, I the mere houseman. It was exhausting work for her, not helped by the bumptious curiosity of Dandelion, last year's foal. We were through by early afternoon but our schedule was in tatters. Preparations for the next day had us flat out until bedtime.

Sunday's tryst was on the Balding gallops close by Watership Down. Leaving the sheep to a neighbour's care, we drove the 80-odd miles eastwards. Two of our children joined us and we had as happy and as eventful a day of it as could possibly be hoped for. Homeward, passing through Whitchurch, I thought of Cassandra Austen and her younger sister, Jane, on girlish errands to those houses 200 years ago. I mused on the cruelty of a fate that makes anyone live farther east than Blandford. And I thought, as I do each spring, how sad it is that our horses, at the peak of fitness, must now come off their fighting rations, laze, overeat and lose their figures. Woody and I will run to fat until mid-July, when a new hunting season will begin to beckon.

By the time the box was unloaded, Tigger had started lambing, and by late bedtime she had produced a pigeon pair. The blackthorn winter, which never seems to fail, was on us; dry but with a cruel east wind. We went to sleep worrying that we should have brought the newest lambs into shelter. We need not have: dawn saw them plump and well as I set off for work.

JULY

Daisy fooled us this year. She dropped her foal in the small hours, some 30 minutes after we had satisfied ourselves that she would not give birth that night. It was only when I went out at half past five, and heard the clatter of little hoofs scrabbling against the stable's wooden inner wall, that I realised what had happened. A little chestnut filly, not quite dry, staggered to her feet – for the first time, I judged – just as I opened the loose-box door.

All seemed to be as it ought to be, and I at least was glad to have been spared the angst of attendance at the lying-in. Bluebell, Bella for short, full sister to Dandelion, thus got off the mark in the opening hours of her life.

There was no excuse for our missing the event. We had hired a foaling alarm, a contraption which, strapped round the mother's neck, detects sweating and sends a signal to a remote receiver by one's bed. It had cried 'wolf' so often, wrecking the night with its raucous importunity, that we had switched it off, putting her slight dampness down to the evening's warmth. She showed no other sign of what was happening, but my wife did say that, when she had left her, just short of four, Daisy turned her head as if to see her off through the stable window. Thus do our animals make monkeys of us: for my own part, I have no doubt that she intended to manage on her own, and I am grateful to her.

AUGUST

Where have our flycatchers gone? Usually, through the summer months a little pyramid of lime under each croquet-hoop records assiduous foraging by a pair, raising one of their two broods. For as long as I can remember they, or their ancestors, have nested in the folded arms of the wisteria. The house wore their nest like a badge, and the comings and goings of the parent birds, and the rearing and launching of their young have been an annual joy. We feel bereft.

They arrived punctually as usual in May, rather early if anything, when the medlar was in flower, and the air was full of the sound of the first silage-cut. I saw them at the old nest site while we were lunching on the lawn, and, as the psalmist said, my heart leapt – it really did. I loved those little birds with their button eyes and perky stance – they seemed like friends. They moused around for a bit while I watched them, and all seemed normal but, as succeeding days passed I realised that they were not nesting in the usual place, and I lost track of them.

In late June, presumably a brood later, they were in evidence again. They actually added an untidy piece of dried grass to last year's nest, and, for a few happy days, they used the handle of the garden roller as a hunting perch: sometimes one was there, sometimes both. Once I saw them mating. But then they disappeared again, not to be seen since.

There was a time when the garden was full of flycatchers every year. I have records of summers when four pairs nested with us. Three on the house, and one in a fruit tree. For years there were always two pairs and now there are none.

Their stays with us – I almost wrote 'their holidays' – were actually periods of frenetic, perilous toil. Perhaps it is for comparative safety that these African birds travel all that way to nest with us in this country? The experts tell us that the motive for migration is a mystery. There must surely be fewer predators in Dorset than in Africa?

However, their stays are not always safe, even here. My mother's diaries show that her cats sometimes took their young, and one year the family that nested by the log-shelter in the kitchen yard lost a parent, hanged on a horse hair. The writer Ernest Thompson Seaton tells of a sparrow killed in this way. I used to think it a piece of macabre artist's licence – now I know better. And two years ago I almost witnessed a sparrowhawk taking the sitting bird from its nest on the house-front. I heard the unmistakable commotion and clamour which always heralds such a raid, and rushed out of the house in time to see the loaded marauder lazily flap away, leaving a trail of feathers and a nest of orphans.

Sadly, there is no avoiding the conclusion that the flycatchers have nested elsewhere this year, because fewer numbers mean wider choice. They can nest more safely away from man. Over the years, I had thought that our flycatchers came to us through preference – even imagined that, in Africa, they looked forward to returning to us, rather as we might think of favourite digs at the seaside. In fact, they have patronised our home all these years *faute de mieux*. But, for whatever reason, that little bit of summer's charm has now gone for ever. We cannot expect to enjoy the close company of our flycatchers again.

Seen from a window, Perdita, framed by the yard gateway, stood at attention, head cocked, looking intently at something on the stones of the stable roof: that something is Pidge. Perdie has plans for Pidge – and they do not include longevity.

Pidge was a visitor whom we did not expect this summer. Attracted no doubt by the familiar signature of the dark arched doorways of our pigeon loft, he (or she?) dropped out of some race, and dropped in on us, seeking company, I presume, and clearly needing rest, food and water. How would he know that we have not kept doves these 20 years?

A beautiful bird – slate and white, with metallic lustres of purple and green on neck and head – he was quite tame. Each shocking-pink leg carried a white ring, which we would have read had we been able to. He very soon got round the women of the house in the matter of handfuls of grain from the fodder room, and pannikins of water. And, equally soon, he became the topic of anxious questions morning and night: 'Is Pidge still with us?', 'Does he look stronger?' and 'Does he watch out for Perdie?'

He left just as he came, without notice. But our imaginings of him back in his northern loft were confounded last week by the discovery that he had merely joined the doves next door.

OCTOBER

Our church is a gem, set in the fields away from the road and apart from the centre of the village. Of course, there must be hundreds like it, and many of greater architectural interest, but to us who live here it is *sans pareille*.

The first, great, Duke of Marlborough spent his infancy in this parish, and must have worshipped here; and the village takes its name from a powerful Norman family that colonised the region, one of whose number lies in full-sized effigy in the Chantry chapel. But it is as the heart of a farming community that it survives and flourishes. That heart is never beating stronger than on the evening of our Harvest Festival, when the church is decorated and full to bursting. It is the same every year, and has been, I dare say, since harvest festivals began.

The oldest part of the building, virtually untouched since it was erected, is the chapel on the southern side, built of knapped flint and Ham stone and dating from the early 1300s; the nave, tower and chancel are of later, but not much later, date. There is a legend, commemorated in ancient tiles in the chapel floor, and in a dozen place-names locally, about a white hart, spotted by King Henry III when hunting nearby, and shot by a local forester contrary to royal fiat. For this misdemeanour local landowners paid a fine, White Hart Silver, as late as 1806. Did I call it a legend? It is history; we just do not know all the details.

One need not be psychic to receive messages from the past in this ancient place. For me it speaks peace and continuity. My sister and one brother were married here, and my father is remembered on the wall by the south door. I love the quiet, the subdued light and the familiar texts and liturgy, and to know that the same words have comforted thousands before me. This is especially poignant at a service after dark, when, seen from the outside, or experienced within, the church and its congregation seem an island of light, sanity and shared goodwill.

Think of us in our little church on an October Friday evening, doing our best to sing the roof off. There is not much grain grown in this corner of the vale – two or three fields at most – and, as it happens, none this year within the parish. Had there been it would have long since been gathered, even in this recent latest of late harvests. But that will not stop us singing, as we do every year, Dix's words, so happily set to Sullivan's music:

Bright robes of gold the fields adorn,
The hills with joy are ringing,
The valleys stand so thick with corn
That even they are singing.

NOVEMBER

Woody has a hang-up about pigs; he probably needs counselling. If he were a human he would provide bread and butter for a psychotherapist who would get him to talk freely about the trauma in his infancy that no doubt accounts for this irrational fear. He could have a good cry about it. Meanwhile, poor chap, he gets little sympathy from me.

One morning late last month, when we had set off in darkness to find hounds who were due to meet in the next parish, I climbed gingerly on board after a mile of leading him, hoping to meet no traffic. Our walk had not been without alarm, at least on my part. A puddle of darker darkness in the road, which my boot had all but brushed in passing, had turned out to be a crouching cat, no doubt returning to the village from his hunting. A smoker's cough from behind a hedge was a sheep, I think. And a mad cackle from the depths of Broad Alders Wood was either an owl going to bed, or a jay waking up – 'Wark, wark, wark,' it said. Woody turned not a hair at any of this, but strode purposefully on. He loves going hunting.

As we climbed Park Lane, leaving the vale behind us, and the first glimpse of dawn showed over the eastern shoulder of Dungeon Hill, the headlights of a considerable vehicle bore down on us. It was a cattle truck, one of those giant three-deckers. 'Where is the market on Tuesdays?' I had just time to ask myself as we cringed in a handy gateway and the thing rumbled past, considerately driven, as most cattle trucks are in these parts. Cheerful lights blazed through the slatted sides as if to belie the misery of its passengers, who announced themselves to our ears and noses as being pigs.

Woody took offence. The truck had passed sufficiently quickly to present no danger, but its odorous wake, dwelling between the high banks of the lane on a windless morning, was like a booster rocket to us. Head up, ears pricked, snorting like a dragon, he fled the scene, oblivious to my wishes. Thanks to the pigs we got to the meet somewhat before hounds that morning.

The people whom we put in County Hall to watch over the officials there have decreed a rubbish dump in the fields at Holnest, close by here. It is to be on the doorstep of several families who have farmed locally for generations, ruining their ancient patrimony, and that of many other, more recent arrivals. In open country, for all to see, a monstrous midden is to be established; a grease-trap for half the county. Everyone knows that a better site could be found, hidden from view, but the Holnest land was covertly purchased by the council, which now means to put it to this purpose willy-nilly.

It is the sort of plan that a zealous, young official in his overheated office might well advance, and be praised for, showing an extreme option – a skittle to be knocked down in committee – part of the dreary round of bureaucratic pipe-dreaming. No sane rural dweller would agree to it, you might suppose. But our council, by a slender margin, has endorsed this nightmare, and a part of our lovely vale, our heritage and home, is to be turned into a squalid, stinking, noisy, ugly, verminous, dangerous hell. (It wasn't, we saw it off!)

❧ 1993 ❧
JANUARY

'Is this land Less Favoured?' 'No, 'tis Severely Disadvantaged.' Thus two farmers, one native, one a visitor from East Anglia, as they plodded over Bodmin Moor. I listened to them on the farming programme early one recent Saturday morning as I enjoyed a mug of tea after giving the horses their breakfast.

It is sad to find that the linguistic sewage of the 'caring professions' has seeped into farming's vocabulary. Let us hope some idiot in Brussels is to blame and that this verbal manure is not home-made. It seems we must talk about a piece of land as if it was sitting beside us in a wheelchair. Who cares? It is just a morass of piffle, but it is sad to find farmer Goodenough from Bodmin paddling in it.

Travelling by train to Exeter, as I do once a quarter, from Dorset, through Somerset into Devon, one can still hear rustic voices. Bustling farmers' wives, off for a day's shopping, get on at Crewkerne, Axminster, or stations farther west, and it is a pleasure to listen to their talk; that is partly why I go by rail. I like to hear the unaffected tones and rich idiom of country people, not obviously related to media-speak or to the muddy argot of our expensively educated children and their peers. The natural local language of the country-bred is, at its best, expressive, colourful, lively and, above all, epigrammatic: it is a treat to hear.

That same farmer Goodenough, reminiscing on the radio about a hard winter on Bodmin when he all but lost his cattle in the snow, said: 'Had it not been for one 'moo!', we'd not have known where they were to.' That seems like poetry to me.

Incidentally, he went on to say, when asked if they hunted on his land: 'They all hunt round here, the North Cornwall, the East Cornwall, and the Bolventor Harriers – if they didn't, God help us with the sheep.' A sentiment I have heard recently expressed in almost exactly the same words by a farmer in North Wales, but I do not ever expect to hear it rendered in agro-bureau speak.

My father had a sort of gardener, who doubled as a sort of groom, who was born at Bockhampton and remembered Thomas Hardy well; he spoke pure William Barnes.[1] He died, if not before the days of television, certainly before it had got its stranglehold on us all. His nerve in late middle life was no better than mine is now. I recall him handing me my father's untried new hunter to hack on to a meet with the words: "'e be too 'igh for I, ye take 'm on Master David.' It was always 'Master David' when Tom wanted something; he was himself already firmly astride my sober pony.

His great joy in life was to go to Sturminster Newton market. When some local farmer needed an extra hand Tom would take a day off, and was a sight to see, both before and after. Market brought out his best attire: highly polished, thick leather gaiters, certainly a clean shirt and collar stud. He always had a drop too much, and came home cap askew and very bold: 'Ye veed varther's horse young David, I be off to Legion.'

Childless, and long since a widower, his must have been a lonely life. He never owned a house while I knew him, but took lodgings here and there. The pub, where, need it be said, the British Legion did its business, was his all in all. A touch quarrelsome, he was still much liked, and people speak to me of him yet, although he has been dead these 20 years. Part of old Dorset died for ever with Tom, but one still strains to hear the echo of his voice.

It is Saturday evening, and today's hunting brought sad intimations of mortality. Woody, my trusty and beloved hunter of six seasons, the soundest, hardiest horse I have ever known, went suddenly, dreadfully lame, when things had been going swimmingly, in the middle of a run. The identical thing happened the previous Saturday, at the same time. Then I put it down to a sudden jar; he was sound when I got him home. Now I have to face the fact that something serious is probably wrong.

We needed to get the horse-box to him, in the middle of nowhere. A kind foot-follower, a familiar figure to me these 40 years, took me in his car while my wife managed the horses, leading Woody gently on to where I should be able to meet her. In the passenger seat was Mr Bairns, now very old, whom I remember so well in his prime – a mad keen hunting farmer who in the immediate postwar years had wonderful big horses out of Ireland, when most of us rode screws. As I edged into the back seat I said 'You remember me, Mr Bairns: the doctor's son?' Of course he did, and we chatted about old times. When they dropped me off, the old man turned to me in parting and said, 'Have you been hunting long in these parts, sir?' Old ways, old manners, old courtesy, old friends with four legs or with two – how they will be missed.

[1] William Barnes (1801–1886) Dorset dialect poet.

MARCH

Here in Dorset it is the season for hunt balls and point-to-points: I can just manage one of each with complacency. To my mind they share with my late London club, now long abandoned, the disadvantage that one is forever bumping into acquaintances at them.

As an official for the first time at our point-to-point this year, I had to take a closer than usual interest in the actual racing – I was time-keeper. Joining the judges on their stand before the first race, I found that the start was invisible from that prestigious spot, hidden behind a covert called Foxpound, familiar from hunting in the area: the course would have been ideal for a ringer in earlier, lawless days. Each race therefore involved getting to a point down the course from where I could clearly see the starter's hectic locale, and then back to my bowler-hatted confrères for the finish. It was rather fun.

Three years ago, our hunt committee took the bold decision to quit Badbury Rings, a shared permanent course where we got a late date and consequently poor entries, for this entirely new site. And this year, for the first time, we risked all in going for an early date. Fortune favoured us with a sunny day, perfect going, large entries and an enormous crowd.

The best and worst part of a point-to-point is usually the hunt race: it holds the most interest for many of us, combined with the least expert competition. My neighbour made a sporting entry on his hunter, Murphy. Carrying 30lb overweight, most of it in his hunting saddle, he trailed from the start, and sensibly pulled up on the second circuit.

As he passed us second time around, the judge turned to me and said: 'That horse is jumping well, anyway.' I could have told him that point-to-point fences must seem child's play to a horse that has gone regularly in our vale. Murphy and his jockey were not short of friends when they started, but I guess that they had gained a few more by the time they had pulled up. Presumably, no one was fool enough to back them.

With three of the races divided because of the heavy entry, the seven scheduled races stretched to ten in all. The sun dropped with the starter's flag in the final race, and we needed headlights as we finally nosed onto the road for Milborne St Andrew, the Piddle Valley and home. After all, it had been a halcyon day. The hunt ball is next week.

March brings other gloomy thoughts to hunting people. Jorrocks's remark, brought against him as evidence before a Commission of Lunacy, 'Hurrah!... it is a frost! The dahlias are dead,' has its counterpart when we see the first of the spring flowers. They were early indeed down in Dorset this year, their poignancy given weight by hunting's uncertain future. How long will it be fore The Jolly Huntsman down the road becomes The Jolly Environmentalist, and what will it be like when we all lead perfectly correct, blameless, risk-free lives?

Once or twice in these pages I have tried to convey to people who feel out of sympathy with it, the charm of hunting. I dare say that I was wasting their time and my own. That noted guru Roger Scruton, a one-time professor of aesthetics, has said: 'No one has really been able to put into words what makes men love hunting'. Perhaps he is right, but, to my way of thinking, Edith Somerville[2] has captured on paper precisely why the sport is so addictive.

It has happened about six times in my life, one of them recently, this season, that I have found myself alone, or virtually so, with a pack of hounds hunting a fox. It happens in my case purely by chance. I have neither the flair nor nerve to shine in the hunting-field, but I have my share of luck.

Just as I once, to my entire surprise, scored a wonderful, long-lofted goal at polo when turning out for the old guard against my late regiment's team, and once, by a random shot, pulled down a pheasant at a great distance in Norfolk.

So, to be alone with hounds, however it has come about, is a feeling never to be forgotten. Something very basic communicates itself from hound to man, and, something quite different in nature, but something, communicates itself from man to horse, as you may see for yourself if you watch a huntsman getting to his hounds on a sticky horse. Perhaps the professor is quite right after all, it defies description. And when I tell you that I prefer not to witness a fox being killed, you will say that it also defies reason. I would agree.

---

[2] Author of *The Experiences of an Irish RM.*

APRIL

St George's Day is more of a watershed in our bucolic world than is either solstice. It is when the imperatives of lambing-pen and stable give way to those of field and garden – animal demands, for a season, taking second place to vegetable insurgence, the green terror of lawn, hedge and weed.

Not that the horses or the sheep can be forgotten. I hate to see hunters shivering and losing condition for lack of a rug at night, as one used to see every year driving to the Badminton Horse Trials when they were held in April. We will be lucky if none of this year's crop of lambs needs the occasional bottle; and there is shearing to be thought of. But St George's Day is when the see-saw of our year tips, as, give or take a day or so, the shameless cuckoo will remind us.

Who does not enjoy the view from an upper-storey window in Paris, or, better still in Florence? Roofscapes have always delighted me, with their unconsidered, jumbled planes of different shades of slate or terracotta and often comic chimney-stacks. I have also always like the unselfconscious backs of houses: unadorned and workaday, they tell you much more about the history of the place than does the propaganda of a smart façade.

Our house has a Georgian front which I am very fond of, but my favourite view is of the straggle of backquarters, descending like a set of ornamental elephants to the stables and an old cowhouse gable-end. The different angles, colours, ages and materials tell of the varied exigencies and interests of succeeding generations of rectors and their broods. The unplanned harmony of the whole is typical of the best of modest, well-mannered English domestic rural architecture. It fits in.

I have come late in life to the love of dogs, or rather to the love of dog. I have told in these pages before of how Perdita, our stray lurcher, came into our lives some two and a half years ago. It is as if a waif had been sent on purpose to soften the heart of a crusty old man, like Little Lord Fauntleroy in the Victorian children's book. Previously, I had thought of a dog as a form of hairy, smelly creature licensed arbitrarily to interrupt one's life and thoughts and costing a great deal of money, like a telephone. But Perdie has become a dear friend and companion.

When we are at weekend family breakfast, Perdie is beside herself with anxiety to know what the plans may be for the day, and whether or not, and to what extent, she is included in them. She lies alert on her beanbag by the Aga, eyeing first my wife and then me, occasionally interrogatively visiting one or other of us with enquiring nose. If either of us should leave the room she darts out into the yard through her flap in the washroom door to set an ambush by the boots in the back porch. In winter, hunting days are black days for Perdita – she knows that she is not included. The best days are when I take the two horses the 20 miles in the lorry to our farrier. The journey, the farrier's dogs, the delicious hoof parings, the all-pervading redolence of rats – the whole thing is heaven to her.

When Perdie and I go out in the morning to feed the young stock and check the sheep in the five-acre field across the lane, she rushes off as we enter the gate, to a perennial rendezvous with an alleged rabbit in the south-boundary hedge: I head at right-angles west to check the level in the water trough. Which done, I whistle, and she comes belting down the hypotenuse, so full of joy, moving as only a long-dog can. A sensation somewhere within my ribcage reminds me why, since time began, poets have located feelings of affection in the heart.

AUGUST

The bindweed climbing the handle of the hoe tells all; I am a reluctant gardener. We have quite a large 'garden', but most of it is down to grass and the responsibility of our small flock of sheep. The two flower-beds, three if you stretch a point, my wife looks after. I just spread compost on them in winter, and, in the spring, plant out snapdragons and the odd tobacco plant. I grow a few 'lady's flowers', as old Tom used to call them – that is, flowers for the house and church – in the end of the vegetable patch, but you cannot call that gardening. Some of our friends' flower gardens and borders make me feel suicidal.

I do grow vegetables, however, and, with the help of the horses, do it rather successfully. Whether it is worth the trouble is often debated, but I enjoy it, and that seems reason enough to me. One does battle of course with the elements, the birds, the insects and slugs, with Perdita even, who thinks that a carefully prepared seed-bed is just the place to bury Friday's bone; but in the end there is always more than we can eat, freeze, or give away.

Most years, a young rabbit moves into the old cow-yard where we have the vegetable patch – it takes up residence under flooring in the open shed where the remnants of last season's hay are usually stacked. I then find myself reluctantly cast in the role of Mr McGregor. I tramp round, leaden-footed, trying to catch the little brute among the garden tools and discarded flowerpots. Perdita is happy to make a positive contribution to this aspect of horticulture. We have never yet caught a rabbit, but, eventually, they seem to decide that there are easier pickings elsewhere and move on. One year, the rabbit mysteriously committed suicide by throwing itself under the wheels of the horsebox, but that is the only time Mr McGregor scored.

My *chef-d'oeuvre* is the asparagus bed. Three years ago, persuaded by my neighbour at some dinner table, a most eloquent lady, I wrote off for a batch of half-grown crowns. I planted and cultivated them by rote, and now we have lots of it: that particular product of my labours is without doubt better than anything one can buy in shops, and worth the minimal labour now involved. It just grows itself, you have only to keep it weeded. 'Where's that hoe?'

The dearth of garden birds gets more noticeable every summer. I find it tragic – no other word will do. It calls to mind the loss of the lovely elms which used to decorate every hedge in our vale. Last year, I told you how the flycatchers, for the first time in my recollection, did not nest in the garden. This year we have barely seen them. There was a sparrow on the lawn the other day behaving like an inexpert flycatcher, trying to fill the void perhaps. For a moment I was deceived, but only for a moment.

Thrushes used to be common here; now they are rare. I saw one of each type at nesting time, but none since. Robins, wrens, all tits, finches and wagtails are down in number and an uncommon sight. Instead, we have magpies, the terrorists of the bird world, and sparrowhawks.

SEPTEMBER

Iron-jawed badgers haunt these parts, but they are preternaturally shy, and, unless you go looking for them, you rarely see one. I met one once, head-on, in a gateway, when out riding. As so often when wild animals behave oddly, he must have been out of sorts – he was lying dead nearby the next time I passed. And once I saw a family playing, at twilight, over the mouth of a culvert by the churchyard. But, otherwise, just the occasional glimpse in headlights is all one sees of them.

But you do not need to see badgers to be aware of them. I can often smell badger in the pickings from the horses' feet after bringing them in from grass on a summer's morning. Perdita loves to go *en brock* – badger smell is like Ma Griffe to her. Why, I do not know. None of the explanations I have heard convince, but she likes nothing better than to pass for a badger on animal radar. She will always roll in badger dung if she can find it, even though it leads to banishment and a scrub under the tap in the stable yard.

Badgers take rights of way seriously; their habitual routes are as inviolable as elephant walks. When, some years ago, I ran sheep netting down one of our hedges, the next morning a badger-shaped hole had been cut on their well-worn track through the hedge. 'Chomp, chomp' it must have gone; I could picture it, making light work of the stout wire. I was reminded of the first thing I learnt of badgers as a child. My father told me they could bite straight through a man's wrist at one go. He would have known, he was a country doctor.

Last autumn, I found a strange wraith of a badger in the old three-seater loo, we call it the 'Holy Trinity', built into the churchyard wall at the bottom of the garden. In one corner, on the ground, was a badger-shaped, badger-coloured sort of nest of binder twine and pied fur. In the failing evening light I thought I was looking at, and smelling, a small, dead badger. But when I cleared the dry debris some months later, not a bone was to be found. It remains a mystery, like many country things, and I am content to leave it so.

As I write, we are enjoying an Indian summer: perhaps when you read this we will be into the equinoctial gales. I love both phases, but these kingfisher, cloudless days are especially precious, not least for the memories they bring: the start of the Michaelmas term at school, when winter uniform felt so hot.

Then there was drilling at Sandhurst, tortured by a Guards Sergeant-Major under the gruelling sun, trying desperately to stand still, focusing on the spire of St Michael's church, and praying not to twitch. 'Mister Hedderson, sir!' he would bellow, 'Why are you dancing around, sir? This is not a ballet school, sir! You are h'idle, sir... take 'is name!' From behind the back rank would come the eldritch shriek of the Drill Sergeant, 'Hofficer Cadet Heggstein, h'idle on parade, sir!' However many times they took my name they never got it right. But there were more memorable names present. From far down the ranks one might hear 'Mister Your Majesty King Hussein, sir, hold your head up, sir!' The irony of it – who has ever had cause to tell that short, proud, lonely, heroic man how to bear himself? We had at least this in common, the King and I, we were both useless on the drill square.

I encountered him only twice during his short stay at the Royal Military Academy. He once asked me the time; someone had to tell me afterwards to whom I had been speaking – I must have been a singularly unaware young man. On the other occasion, I followed him round the twisting Surrey and Berkshire lanes as we learnt to ride motorcycles. It was a wicked winter, and I remember thinking how well that son of the desert stood the cold.

DECEMBER

For as long as I can remember, there have been horses to be clipped in the Christmas holidays. Clipping is perhaps the worst of the winter stable chores. Perfectionists clip every few weeks through the hunting season; we normally do it three or possibly four times, with the last clip timed to have our string looking at its best for Boxing Day. After Christmas we tend to let the coat grow out, ready for the moult, and to leave the emerging summer coat untouched.

Although clipping has a lot to do with a horse's looks – I am told that dandies used to shave their horses – it is in fact essential if a horse is to be worked hard and kept clean and in good condition. A horse's winter coat is not made for running about in. It has to come off – a process almost impossible without a bit of magic.

Twitching – and I do not refer to bird-watching – is a mystery. How is it that by gripping a horse's upper lip firmly you can almost instantly tranquillise him? I find the scientific explanation unsatisfactory. Endorphins are released into the bloodstream when you twitch a horse, they say: one is still left wondering how and why.

For the benefit of those not familiar with this everyday miracle of the stable yard, a twitch is a small loop of soft rope of much the same gauge as sash-cord, but more flexible, and of about the circumference of a saucer. Usually, it is attached to a short length of broomstick, although other levers are used nowadays; the loop passes through a hole drilled about half an inch from the end of the stick. You place the loop round the mobile bobble that forms a horse's upper lip and rotate the stick until the loop becomes a ligature. Bingo! In nine cases out of ten, the horse seems to go half asleep and you can do anything with him – the effect seems almost hypnotic.

It is possible to get a similar result by seizing and twisting the loose flesh on a horse's neck. Gypsies do this, I am told. But it takes a large, strong hand, and probably a small horse, for it to work. I have tried it, and managed it, sometimes.

But the real mystery of twitching is not why it works, but why it does not hurt. Try to do anything uncomfortable to a horse and the animal will tell you quickly enough if it does not like it – their memories are phenomenal; they forget nothing. Yet my great half-ton monster Woody, whom I cannot approach with an aerosol because he thinks that the hissing noise is a snake, and who once threw me boldly across the box when I was unwise enough to grip his foot between my thighs to free my hands to dress a nasty wound, stands like a lamb to have the twitch put on when I come to clip his ears and head.

There are a lot of equestrian experts about these days. I refer, of course, not to old buffers who have spent a lifetime in and out of stables and maybe commanded a cavalry regiment, but to the likes of Miss da Vinci at the riding school. Miss da Vinci, who looks to be 15 years old or so, is an Assistant Instructor, or 'AI', and gives the impression of having been present at the creation of the equine species. There is more knowledge of such things in her little finger... and what a very little little finger it is.

I have never, to the best of my knowledge, met an Instructor – an 'I' – although I am told that these exalted beings exist. I feel that Burke's praise of Marie Antoinette would hardly suffice to describe such a creature.

Miss da Vinci often puts me right, and I am very grateful (as you can see). It is she who, if she rides my horse, will leave the bridle so scientifically trussed that it looks like some caliph's cipher and takes ten minutes to sort out. And it is she who would put three rugs on Woody where one suffices, if I should let her; and would bandage him up like the invisible man for even the shortest journey in the horsebox.

Much as I do, Woody holds Miss da Vinci in high regard. When she rides him it will be in the manège, a place I never set foot in willingly, and he tucks his head in, picks his feet up and generally looks worth twice what I paid for him. The tiny polymath on Woody is like a robin on a round of beef – he does not give much change from 18hh – but she certainly knows how to ride.

⁕ 1994 ⁕
FEBRUARY

As I was reminded on a recent, rare and reluctant visit to London, there was a time when you could get breakfast on the up-train. I recall this as being one of the pleasures of adolescence. The stewards, attentive and busy, smart in their red and blue monkey-jackets, would recognise you, or seem to do so; it made you feel a man. You reached London with a good opinion of yourself; the eggs fed the ego as it were. It was expensive – grumbling about the cost was part of the ritual, but it was a luxury worth paying for.

A small buffet has started up at our station, where there was never one before, at least not in my memory. A Scottish family, whom I secretly name the McSporrans, entrepreneurs if ever there were, will proudly give you breakfast while you wait for your train, at a cost of £1.99. This is too good to last, of course – note that I am careful not to identify the station – officialdom will soon catch up. The McSporrans will be picked off by a hygiene patrol for not having six wash-basins, or for serving real food that people enjoy eating.

'Tax inspector, tax inspector, tax inspector.' I wish I could think of a more congenial lyric to match the music of my horse's metalled feet as he walks out at exercise, but the accents are precisely right; try it your-self. A horse's paces boggle the mind if you attempt to analyse them. The walk is like that of a pantomime horse, the two actors being out of step and out of time with each other, like an awkward Dad's Army squad. As the leader steps off, (as Woody does), with the left, or near fore, the back-end follows with the right, not quite hitting the same beat. The accent is on the two front feet, the first the strongest. The hind legs, which do so much work in faster paces, and in jumping, step quite lightly.

Our walk takes us past some cattle, patently in the wrong field; they look challengingly at us, as strays will. Turning in at the next farm entrance, and craning over the yard gate, I cry 'Miss Roberts'. She receives the unwelcome message, giving me the kindliest smile. She and I must be much of an age; we have grown up in the same scattered parish, but I believe that those are the first words, apart from 'good morning', that I have ever spoken to her. Yet we each know precisely who the other is. She is to be seen, with her sister, on the roof of their cattle byre, enjoying the hunt when the hounds come by. I am no doubt 'Doctor's son', although it is a quarter of a century since my much-loved father died.

MARCH

Perdita, autocrat of all our arrangements, has decreed a bone-mountain in the kitchen garden. Every Friday brings the butcher's van, and Perdie knows it: she knows the very note of its engine. Before now, she has belted away from me as I ride up the drive, on picking up its sound, and I would arrive in the stable yard just in time to see her slink off in the direction of the broccoli, rolling a sheepish eye at me. If I should follow her she will postpone the interment – secrecy seems to be part of the ritual – but, otherwise, palpably longing to gnaw it, she will instead bury her prize. She must be driven by the strongest of instincts.

Before I had properly thought the matter through, I used to think it very clever of her to remember where all her bones lay hidden. For, long after she had buried it, the bone whose time had come would be exhumed, probably from an immaculate seed-bed. But, of course, memory does not come into it: she sees and hears with her nose.

An outdoor life and early hours are usually at war with watching television. I am, however, mildly addicted to Miss Marple and her confrères, but when a classic novel is screened I become completely hooked – everything has to give way to watching the next episode or its repeat.

The great thing with these occasional treats is not to expect the impossible: how could anyone visually reproduce a great literary work, and in six hours? If the series just manages to give the true flavour of its model that is a great deal, and quite enough to make the enterprise worthwhile. The recent screening of *Middlemarch* was a good deed in a naughty world – well done the BBC.

Of course, there were cracks in the make-up – all of us no doubt spotted our own, it is part of the fun. But surely there was someone who read the script, or who was in earshot during rehearsals, who knew that, neither then nor now, would a Dr Lydgate refer to his clerical friend as 'Revd Fairbrother'? But it was, as ever, with horses that they got most adrift. It is safe enough to bring on vintage cars, old coal-fired engines and antique rolling-stock, to give colour to a period scene, but few actors look easy in the saddle – you cannot simulate good hands and seat. No wonder that TV horses usually rear; and the obligatory neigh, presumably added by the sound-effects department, is, at least in my experience of this unsettling caper, also quite out of place.

MAY

There is no more satisfying moment in the outdoor year than when our fields are newly rolled. For a few days they look like brushed baize. It does them good, and it does me good: I feel that spring is really on the way.

I question that there ever has been a time when spring hung fire as it seems to have done this year. As I write, the first swallow has arrived, wasted from its long journey, and looking lost, regretful and homesick, and the cuckoo was right on cue, on St George's Day. By the time you read this, we shall no doubt have at last turned the long-awaited corner of the seasons, but what a wait it has been.

April was appalling. When the wind was not south-westerly and wet, it was somewhere in the northern quarter, and when there was no wind, as like as not we had a frost. It was a cruel time for animals that had wintered out and must have been pining for the first bite of new grass. Farmers who had the misfortune to lamb out-of-doors in April have had a terrible time of it. We, luckily, had our first crop in the much kinder March – this was unplanned, but it worked out well for us: they were skipping and on top of life before April struck.

One morning, early in the month, as I was driving to work, I saw that an old friend, a pony whom I have glanced at in passing almost daily for seven years, was lying dead in his field. Nothing looks deader than a dead horse, there was no mistaking the case, and I felt a wrench in my chest as I hurried on. Coming home that evening, the dragged and trampled grass reminded me also that nothing better illustrates the term 'dead-weight'.

He had had a happy retirement I judged, and there must be worse ways for a horse to die than just to fade out on a cold, unseasonal morning, waiting for spring to come. I went to enquire after him a fortnight later. He must have been born unexpectedly early, like our lambs, because, as I then discovered, his improbable name was April. As our local poet had it, writing just a parish or so away from April's field, 'In my beginning is my end' (*East Coker*, T.S. Eliot).

A couple of days after April's death we took ourselves off to the warmth of the French Alps, to ski in the Trois Valées. Not having been on the slopes for more than ten years, it was reassuring to find that, after a few shaky minutes, my original level of make-do incompetence returned and I could get round well enough to enjoy the freedom of the mountainside. Of course, there is nothing natural about skiing on a prepared piste, nor anything truly adventurous to it, but there is something bird-like and liberating in looking down from the mountain top to the village below, and knowing that you can, unaided, make your way down there, and in no time at all. It has a lot in common with hunting.

JULY

Like Prospero's island, this house is full of noises. The other morning I woke up to a muffled throbbing in the chimney (did not Edgar Allan Poe write a tale about a heartbeat below the floorboards?). There was nothing for it but to flee the place; after all, what is a stuck starling or a jammed jackdaw compared with the dead burglar a friend recently discovered in the chimney of her house in France? Country life all too often turns suddenly into a horror story.

More benign noises come from the mice who have the freedom of the place. I swear that one of them polishes its family's shoes above my bed-head in the early mornings, and all of them practise hop-skip-and-jump, vertically, in the wall cavities. Bats in the bedroom are commonplace; you feel their presence rather than hear their arrival. *Pace* the Community Bat Facilitator, or whatever high functionary defends the beneficiaries of that particular fad of our rulers, stout gardening gloves and a tennis-racket deal with bats.

A hedgehog once announced its presence by rattling the cellar door alarmingly, late one night. It had presumably fallen through the coal-hatch grating, and climbed the almost vertical steps to seek freedom: hedgehogs are determined creatures. My mother found a lizard in her kitchen last week, and there are always toads, frogs and newts in the cellar.

Old houses, as well as harbouring errants and squatters, occasionally yield treasure. Beneath bedroom wallpaper we have just found a scrap from *The Times* of 24 June 1864, jet black on white and pristine, it might have been delivered yesterday (if *The Times* were not printed grey on grey nowadays). It was a fragment of the parliamentary report from the previous day.

Lord Paget was on his feet explaining why the loading of three troop-carriers bound for Dublin with the 60th Rifles had been adjusted so that all the families travelled together: 'to prevent inconveniences that would be occasioned to the women and children to be embarked.' One wonders if the 60th had a particularly vocal wives' club, or if, thinking of *Vanity Fair*, there was a Mrs Colonel O'Dowd in the case. The scrap is covered up again now, for someone else to rediscover.

I woke early last Sunday morning – as I seem to do without trying when we have ewes in lamb – and gave myself a few minutes to surface. It was a mistake. When I got out to Wimp, she was lying help-less, heavy with lamb and 'cast' against a tree trunk. Something had attacked her. There was a small wound in her flank, and a yard-long, fatal v-shaped stitch of her gut glistened on the ground. You could almost picture the cruel tooth or beak that had just dropped it. I guess I was only seconds too late. Poor love, she was distressed, but not, I think, in much pain, and my arrival, and that later of my wife, will have comforted her. She had known no other parents and always seemed to crave our company.

Not so many years ago I could have shot her with my father's old army pistol, but the law, so prompt in its exactions on the law-abiding, has made utility gun ownership virtually impossible, except, of course, for gang-sters. My neighbour, Michael, who is a gamekeeper, did the deed. If you wonder what one does with a large carcass on a hot, sunny Sunday, the answer is simple – you ring the kennels. No doubt the authorities will make that simple resort to self-help and common sense impossible too before we are much older.

Wimp came to us in 1986 when we purchased a batch of orphans. She was the runt of quads or triplets – 'You can have that one for nothing.' – but she survived and thrived, and grew to be enormous and belie her name. A perfect mother, she gave birth without assistance, fed generously, and had, in all, ten lambs, all boys bar two. The one daughter whom we kept, Dotty, is giving birth in the orchard as I write, attended by my wife. Thus, country life goes on.

AUGUST

If Perdita has a favourite hymn it must be 'New Every Morning', even though her 'hopes of heaven' are no more than the next bone, or actually catching the rabbit in Chantry Mead. The freshness with which dogs greet the routine of each dawning day, the ease with which they are pleased, and, above all, their uncritical worship of 'master' make them themselves adorable.

Dung-struggling as I call it, is a summer chore that cannot be avoided by those who do not have the acreage to match their stable, and who must therefore be especially careful to keep their grass clean and free of parasites. An extension of Parkinson's Law seems to ensure that the number of horses owned increases until it exceeds the grazing available. Put more simply, you always have one too many of them. So, every day in summer, wet or shine, some time must be spent patrolling the paddocks with fork and barrow, and trundling the stuff away.

As anyone who has had horses on his land knows, they are the most wretched grazers. Left to themselves they will soon have any grassland disfigured by overgrown rank patches, which they would rather starve than eat from. Horse-sick land is an eyesore, and a dreadful waste. The answer, of course, lies in cross-grazing. Keep just a few sheep, say one or two per acre, and they put all to rights. They eat everything, including young docks and thistles in the spring, and their winkle-picker feet and inoffensive droppings work wonders with the soil.

If you keep sheep you must fence the land properly – no short cuts – and, like horses, sheep must be looked at every day, and must be drenched and have their feet inspected regularly. I cannot pretend that they are not hard work, but the rewards in terms of the look of the place well repay the effort. Paradoxically, the extra mouths double the horse-grazing capacity of the land, and the cheque we have just received for this year's lamb crop will take care of the farrier's bills for the best part of three months.

Backing Dandelion has been one of the events of the summer. Dandy is the first of the two foals we had from our old Irish hunter, Daisy; his full-sister is called Bluebell, or Bella. Dandy is now a bright and sparky three-year-old. When he was only six weeks, he jumped the gate out of his field one night; we gelded him early, and we have handled him almost daily all his short life. He is biddable, and seems to love human company, but actually getting into a saddle on his back did make me slightly pensive.

I need not have worried. He took the whole performance as being entirely natural, merely turning his neck so as to inspect, and then to nibble, the toecap of my boot.

OCTOBER

This small village seems to be a place of importance to swallows; they muster here for migration. The first enormous batch gathered and were gone early in September; they will mostly be in their winter quarters now. Their small rear-party are departing as I write.

My Uncle Horace, writing from Natal at this time two years ago, reported that they go about in large flocks, in areas where there happen to be suitable insects to feed on, sometimes he sees hundreds if not thousands of them resting on the telephone wires...

He owed his love of birds to a Norfolk boyhood, and his name, properly Horatio, to his birthplace. It happened that the third Lord Nelson was visiting Burnham Thorpe parsonage when he was born. One can picture the scene – the noble equipage on the gravel sweep, the doctor's gig nearby, the kitchen alive with the excitement of the double event, the midwife with her pot of tea perhaps, and the visitor's servants lording it over the local bumpkins. From what I know of my grandparents, neither the young rector nor his wife at the seventh lying-in (she was to have eleven) would have been phased; they were a resourceful couple – they had to be.

Young Horry got his schooling, like his two brothers, at Brighton College, his six sisters went to Roedean. Originally intended for university and the law, he was in fact taken early out of school and sent to South Africa, with his elder brother George, under the 1820 Settlers Scheme. Apart from two short visits, half a century apart, he did not see the country of his birth again.

After two years' hard graft as a student, he started up on his own, with sheep; then he headed north, got land in Natal, worked extremely hard, prospered, and raised a family. It is an old story, a younger son sent off with empty pockets to seek his fortune; and making good.

If he had lived another year, this uncle, whom I never knew, would have been 90. He would perhaps have had a fellow-feeling with our arriving swallows, and I do not doubt, would have given a passing thought this month to his great namesake at sea off Trafalgar.

It is bewildering to lose a landmark. For all of my lifetime, and no doubt much longer, a small shed has stood in a field near here, which I often passed on horse or foot; last week it had gone. It was not a thing of beauty, but it stood centrally, at the height of the field, once straddling a much older hedge, which it had survived. My ancient map shows the hedge, but not the shed. It was partitioned internally so as to provide a stable in each field: a door connected them. It must have been a godsend when shuffling stock between the two pastures. It had a prefabricated oak frame, and was clad with corrugated-iron – factory-built, I guess, bought from a catalogue, delivered by wagon, and erected, with much head-scratching, by the estate carpenter.

Long disused and not on the way to anywhere, it can have been seldom visited, but I used to sneak up there once or twice a year to feel its atmosphere, and speculate about its past. What I particularly liked were the long wooden rollers mounted on all the door jambs to prevent animals barking their hips when squeezing in and out – testament to the thought given to the care of livestock.

Visiting the site before it was ploughed over, standing there, rather sadly, early in the morning, I looked for a memento of an old friend. The low, sniping sun caught a flash of glass – a bottle, slender, pale green, irregular in shape, and with a bubble caught in its side, it had in raised writing on one side 'Carton's HP Sauce'.

It did not take long to guess its provenance. Not relish for a cowman's snap, but a drenching bottle – pinched from his wife's kitchen, I do not doubt – the handy shape, the long, strong spout, and the safely rounded mouth would have made it just the ticket for dosing an ailing calf (no sheep on this low-lying land in those days). It must have been mislaid, certainly not discarded, trodden underfoot, lost in straw bedding in dim lamplight, regretted and replaced. I shall have the deepest satisfaction in putting it to the same use again.

✣ 1995 ✣
JANUARY

The latest daffy make-work scheme to be handed down by the com-
mittee-men and bureaucrats who are apparently licensed to harass us
in any way that pleases them, involves the registration of the few pet
sheep who mow our orchard and keep the pasture sweet. I believe that
the next step is for them to be brutally ear-tagged and numbered. What
possibly purpose can this serve, apart from providing employment for
people in distant, over-heated offices, and pabulum for their computers?
Why should they be allowed to wring the last drops of carefree style and
independence out of country life, and do it at our expense?

I always name our sheep when I first see them. Something about the
circumstance of their arrival, or birth, or about their physical appearance,
prompts the process. When Gloria, the original matron of our flock, first
trotted into our orchard, her old head cocked on one side the better to see
out of her one good eye, anxiously following my young shepherd neighbour, who was carrying her lambs, there was something so ineffably
blowzy about her that I did not hesitate a moment; and I apologise to all
the chic, svelte, aristocratic Glorias who may be reading this – the name
means 'barmaid' to me. If it is any consolation to them, I was to become
very fond of Gloria.

As Jane Austen has said, and repeated several times in different words:
'There is so much of gratitude or vanity in almost every attachment.'
Gloria stole my heart by the way she would walk out of the very middle
of the flock to me when I called to her, when she had temporarily rejoined
her original extended family on annual honeymoon. The same authority
would have been quick to point out that I always had a bucket in my hand.

Already old and half-blind when she arrived, she stayed with us for about
three years, and then, early one morning, when we had been waiting anxiously for her to give birth, I found her with a single, very large, dead ram
lamb beside her. I do not know how it is, but one often seems to betray
one's pet animals at their end, or feel that one has done so. It was a
Sunday morning, but nonetheless, my friend the rector got his friend the
kennel-lady to come with a gun and give Gloria her quietus. I still grieve
a little for her.

Have I told you enough to make you share my resentment that some

– 45 –

distant feather-bedded office person, operating some feather-headed scheme, should claim a share in what goes on between my sheep and me?

I only once made a sound investment. About the time that Gloria died, we had a windfall. With infinite care, and on the best advice, a balanced investment portfolio was constructed; a little flutter here and a lot of ballast there, the whole thing was skilfully 'crafted', as people (tiresome people) would say, and absolutely copper-bottomed, brass-bound and water proof. Black Monday followed within weeks, if not days, of the perfection of this proud City artefact, and I lost the bulk of it.

However, I had kept in hand the purchase price of two horses such as I had never previously been able to afford, one each for myself and for my wife: as I write, they are munching contentedly in the stable. Older, slower and naughtier than in their brilliant youth (who isn't?), their capital value all but written-off, they have paid dividends 'beyond the dreams of avarice'.

MARCH

'Goodbye' to Taunton, where I have worked for the past eight years, and soon shall work no longer. 'Tarnt'n' is what some of the old school still call the county town of Somerset – they throw the word at you with a quizzical twinkle, as if to say, 'Surely you know that people like us pronounce it so?' – but in fact the old usage is not the shibboleth it was. 'Tarnt'n' has become merely a password among a few dozen of the older families, relic of an idea that once flourished and now dies: it would be interesting to know its origin.

As a schoolboy I conceived a passion for Somerset's buccaneering county cricket side. As soon as I could drive, and could command use of a car, I would travel the 40 miles of then wiggly road to Taunton, to watch Gimblett bat and Hazel bowl.

Taunton itself has not changed much in the near decade that I have intimately known it. I like it as much as I find it possible to like a town; even though my work, which was with addiction problems, disclosed its seamier side for daily close inspection. For light relief, I took most of my annual holiday on winter Tuesdays, following a favourite pack of foxhounds. I do not know what others may have made of this schizophrenic life: for my own part, I found the two contrasting views of twentieth-century life enlivening.

My two happiest memories of Taunton are of a piano player in the High Street – Chopin in the open air; and the Women's Institute market in Bath Place. Here, on Wednesdays or Fridays, I could stock up with marmalade, and listen to the country ladies' gentle *badinage*.

My wife seems to have acquired a follower in the shape of the ram, Sammy, who comes to us annually, on loan, after what you might call his professional engagements. Charollais lack presence, as rams go, being squat, and rather shabby in appearance; but Sammy has the most amazing jumbo-humbug eyes, and is not without appeal.

He walked out on our ewes a week ago, and was found, after two days of anxious search, happily camping in the churchyard. Enticed into our adjacent orchard, he was thence removed by his owner. Passing him in his new quarters, out riding, my wife unwisely called to him, and this morning he came hobbling up the drive. As I write, he is again munching daffodils in the orchard.

APRIL

Daffodils, the trumpets of spring, have come in several bars too early this year – according to our score, at least: we have a wedding here next month. Instead of the golden blaze that we had hoped for we will have tiresome knots of dying leaves, which the strimming hand twitches to remove. I am much too impatient to be any sort of gardener.

If daffodils are its heralds, surely lambs are the favourite children of the spring? Riding out this morning, with the usual complement of a led horse and Perdita, my route was through my neighbour's field, aptly named Stonylongs. It was early, but last night's lambs had already been visited. They and their mothers were a bit sorry for themselves as we had just had a sudden short tropical downpour, the umpteenth 'last straw' of the wettest winter anyone round here can remember – the good effect of two rare dry sunny days undone in a minute it seemed (how ever shall we get a roller onto the paddocks in time to park the wedding cars?) but in fact, at this time of year the water-table is inexorably dropping, the new, so demoralizing, puddles will quickly drain.

I knew that the lambs had been visited because, although they had not yet been ringed, they had had numbers sprayed on their little flanks. I had never seen this before, in this particular flock, but it is, I suppose, the implementation of some new crazy rule. Number 28 I noticed seemed to be in difficulties, trapped in a chaos of fallen poles by a practice jump. I turned back, and, and, typically, my great booby of a horse, who weights all of a ton, jibbed at this little chewed, damp morsel and would not close with it. However our approach had the desired effect, 28 was inspired to extricate himself, and scampered gladly off bleating to his mother.

Who is it who needs to know that twins were born to 28's mama in Stonylongs, in the parish of Glanvilles Wootton, early this spring morning? Where will that number fly to, on what screens will it figure, and, above all, why; and what does it cost, and who will pay? Have we gone quite mad that we allow office people to batten on us in this way?

I am tempted to say that surely nothing could be sillier than registering new-born lambs, but I know all too well that something even sillier will follow. Perhaps next spring we will be counting daffodils. Our world seems to have exchanged a god before whom not one sparrow was forgotten for a tyrannical idol of omniscience.

If there is a greater pleasure, apart from singing it, than listening to oratorio it has eluded me. Earlier this month we attended a joint school performance of Haydn's *Creation* – it was spell-binding, I was on the edge of my seat almost from start to finish. I say 'almost', because I do not think that there is any work of that duration that does not have the occasional *longueur*, if one is honest. And the da capa, and repetition of phrases, typical of work of that period, but less used by Haydn than some of his contemporaries, can be irritating. 'Get on with it' one feels like saying, 'We heard that the first time'.

Less great than Bach, less brilliant that Handel, Haydn's music is I think consistently happier than that of either. He was a countryman by birth, of peasant stock, a good shot and fisherman, and all these qualities shine through his setting of familiar passages from Milton and the Bible. His *Creation* is truly something to be heard in the countryside, and in the spring.

An old friend, by chance, took the place beside me. No stranger to these pages, she was a superb point-to-point jockey when I first knew her nearly half a century ago. We have met often hunting, and more recently at the bridge table, and she has just been widowed. We collogued, quietly, when the music allowed, and, as we followed the libretto in our programmes, jointly enjoyed the depiction of the living natural world that came to us, over the gap of the centuries, from Milton, via Croatia, and these children's voices to the great nave of Milton Abbey.

It is permitted to stepfathers to boast about their borrowed children. I brag shamelessly of mine, who are as clever as they are good-looking: both are very bright. But when, as a father only of sons I have no right to expect, I take my beautiful youngest 'steppy' on my arm, and walk the few paces through the orchard to our jewel of a church, I shall not be fussing about precocious daffodils.

JUNE

Midsummer is when we usually get in hay, but this is no normal year – the grass just has not grown as it ought: we have had two false springs. A farmer told me, out hunting, after the first warm spell, that the young grass had been frosted when it was 'nesh', and that it would not start again in a hurry. I learnt from Chambers, that evening, that nesh is a dialect word from Old English meaning, among other things, soft, crumbly and tender. I had heard the word used before, but never fastened onto it. Like so many country words it is onomatopoeic, its sound suggests its meaning. What else could nesh mean but soft and tender.

The second false spring brought on the daffodils too early, as I complained when I last wrote on this page: we had wanted them to be at their best for my stepdaughter's wedding. Since then, we have had several harsh frosts, and really no spring weather to speak of at all, and the grass just has not got away – except, of course, where it is not wanted.

However, my private bet is that, despite the present gloom of the kind neighbours who usually let us have some hay, things will lurch back to normal, and we shall get the 400 bales we need, to keep four horses comfortably through the winter, and leave a little over.

The limes that we keep finding about the place, and which the mower grumbles at ferociously, are not evidence of some wonderful new initiative from Brussels – the 'North Dorset Citrus Regime' perhaps – but reminders of a recent wedding. They featured, on sticks, in all the flower arrangements, but popped off, and rolled away to their several hiding places, when these were being dismantled.

If I were to tell you that our family wedding was a great success you would smile and yawn – what wedding is not a triumph? However, it has left me with three special memories.

That morning, during one of several anxious visits to the church, I saw the head flower-arranger – who, with her flowers, had come from Kenya – standing in stockinged feet on the altar, with a lily in her hand, when a rare ray of sunlight suddenly struck through the stained-glass window behind her, and it looked for all the world as if she had just stepped out of it.

There was also the moment when, standing by the grandfather clock in the hall, just as my father must have waited for my sister more than 40 years ago, and as many fathers must have stood before, anxious, all too aware of the clock's message, I first saw the bride, at the turn of the stair.

And then, when we had passed the dead-headed daffodils in the orchard, successfully dodging the showers, met my friend the rector in his billow- ing robes, and followed him into the church, came a real surprise, some- thing I was entirely unprepared for. The whole congregation turned, with a kindly, wondering stare, and fixed their eyes on the girl on my right arm.

AUGUST

Waiting nervously in a great man's ante-room the other day I was for a moment puzzled to hear his transatlantic secretary seem to say, more or less, 'Mr Ogre, there is a rider waiting to see you'. She wasn't far off the mark: nearly everything I write in these pages, and elsewhere, is composed on horseback. The steady rhythm of a favourite horse's walk, its silent company, and that of Perdita, and the Dorset countryside, seem to help sort my thoughts into order.

I always turn towards the downs, and climb, aiming to see more of the rim of the great bowl we live in; that skyline is full of story and history, and of course memories. I need not climb far to get a distant view north to Alfred's tower at Stourhead. A brisk ride westwards would bring Admiral Hardy's monument in sight, and the Cross in Hand would be on my route, that enigmatic stone and bleak spot where Tess of the D'Urbervilles came face to face with destiny.

'Shall you break them in yourself?' my wife and I are often asked, in reference to the two young horses, Daisy's progeny, who are now of an age to enter on the serious business of their lives. I always reply that 'break' hardly seems the right word, although there may be breaks of a different sort to come. Both of them have been handled regularly since birth, and, apart from the odd hiccup, neither has taken the least bit of serious notice of the various gradual steps of bringing them into work. Backing them, that supposedly traumatic moment when one first climbs gingerly into the saddle, and which we did with both of them last year, was a non-event.

The most difficult thing we have encountered is to get free forward move-ment, in the desired direction, with a rider on board: long-reining seems to be the answer. You walk behind the horse, rather like an old-fashioned ploughman, urging it forward, and teaching it to accept directional instructions from the reins – then try riding it again. I am firmly convinced that, anyway in the case of our two youngsters, it is purely a question of their understanding what is wanted of them; they seem to long to do it.

Second only to backing a young horse, riding him out on the roads for the first time is perhaps the most exciting moment; something akin to a test flight I suppose. Dandelion the four-year-old, the older of the two, took me down to the village Post Office a fortnight ago. Since then, almost every day, we have gone here and there together, increasing his experience and our mutual trust, and getting to know each other's body language. No doubt we will have our problems, but, to date, 'breaking' Dandy has been pure joy, making this a summer to remember.

SEPTEMBER

Experts love to put you down. How often have I not carried home in my head, ever and again repeating it to myself, aloud, like a half-wit, so as to keep it lodged there, the detail of the plumage and flight of some unrecognised and supposedly rare bird, only to find that the handbook lists it as 'commonly found throughout the British Isles'. Usually its name is an added insult – my 'rarity' is a lesser drab-feathered ditch-twit, or some such.

Last week I brought back to the house for identification a rather fetching yellow flower that I had found in the paddock. I was confident that it was not, but it might just have been, ragwort, a menace to livestock at all times, but never more so than when there is little else left to graze. Its burst of small sun-like flowers suggested a name such as little dauphin, or perhaps dairymaid's delight. Not a bit of it – it was common fleabane. In one swipe the taxonomist, looking down his scientific nose, managed to belittle both the flower and its finder. What this plant does to fleas one can only guess from its Latin name – *pulicaria dysenterica*; evidently it sends them hopping.

I have another flower book which I am much fonder of; I do not know where it came from, or how it got onto my shelves, but the date pencilled in the flyleaf is 1928, and it is called *The Children's Book of Wild Flowers*. It is beautifully illustrated, no doubt by someone's maiden aunt, and the text gives the mythology and folklore associated with flowers' various names, and their medicinal uses. It is a book after my own heart and a treasured possession.

Fleabane is not described, but a flower that I know well, yarrow, is. Yarrow, which looks a bit like miniature cow parsley, has small parasols of tiny white flowers, and the most delicate many-fingered leaves. It grows only as high as it needs to, to get a share of the sun, and it twinkles amongst the burnt grass everywhere in our pasture, and even on the lawn. In a few weeks it will beckon my quickening pace as I mistake it once again for a mushroom.

Yarrow I learn is also called devil's nettle (try brushing its leaf against your face), nose-bleed, staunch-grass or carpenter-grass (for its styptic property), milfoil, wild-pepper or old-man's-pepper (sniff it), and old-man's-mustard, but 'In some parts of the west of England children call it bunch-of-daisies or angel-flower', well done them I say. Yarrow is also said to answer a very important question:

> *If a person takes one of the leaves, turns it round inside his nose and all the while thinks of his sweetheart, and at the same time repeats:*
>> *Green yarrow, green yarrow, you bear a white blow;*
>> *If my love loves me, my nose will bleed now;*
>> *If my love don't love me, it won't bleed a drop;*
>> *If my love does love me, 'twill bleed every drop.*

I have not tried this, but am rather past that sort of thing – 'blow' means bloom, of course.

OCTOBER

Autumn's litany is almost ended. The leaves, which, thanks to the drought, started to fall as early as July, hang on, and the maize still stands in the fields waiting to go for silage, and there are some apples to be gathered, but mostly the year's harvest is complete. The hay, hard to come by, early and expensive, is sheeted up against the wet south-westerly gales, and grain stores everywhere are full to bursting.

Linseed was the last crop to clear my neighbour's fields. Then the last of the great square-bodied grain lorries, so terrifying to meet on horseback, quit our lanes, to be replaced by the equally menacing, but better managed ploughs. I do not know who drives the grain trucks, but they are not local people, and they seem unconscious of the fear that they instil. The ploughs, laughably called 'reversible' (how could you possibly reverse a plough – they mean 'two way'), great double banks of shining blades behind a gigantic tractor, are truly terrifying things to meet in a narrow place.

I have become rather attached to linseed. I enjoy the swathes of blue flowers in the spring, so much easier on the eye than the garish yellow yell of oilseed rape. By July, as it stands almost ready to be harvested, it hisses and rustles pleasantly as you walk by, each small spherical pod holding its neat batch of seed like a tiny fist. Perhaps the hiss is a warning. Linseed is lethal to animals if not properly prepared before being fed; and I have been told that, in bulk, in store, the seed is as dangerous as quicksand – you can drown in it.

Very soon we shall be decorating the church for the Friday evening Harvest Festival, followed by supper in the Village Hall. Ours is not a beautiful village; apart from the church, and one or two of the older houses, it is, in aesthetic terms, a rather regrettable sprawl of inter-war and postwar brick and worse. But it has a human heart and spirit that must be enviable. I have often tried to put my finger on the secret of this harmony, and I can come no closer to it than to say that nearly all contribute and join in, and no one throws his or her weight around more than is tolerable. We seem to have a shared sense of propriety; it is seen at its best when we sit down together for our annual Harvest Supper.

Woody, the great leonine chestnut Irish hunter, who is the apple of my eye and boon companion, may be entering on his final season:

he is, as they say, on his last legs, poor chap. For some time now we have nursed him along, at first using a very expensive drug ('powdered banknotes' I call it), which improves the circulation to the feet; latterly we have resorted also to that universal standby 'bute' (Phenylbutazone). No one should think that there is cruelty involved, it is merely a question of making his feet comfortable. But 'bute' dulls feeling all over, and a horse of Woody's size and determination cannot be safely managed amongst the excitements of the hunting field with more than a minimum dose inside him and a deadened mouth – as I discovered on the only occasion that he ever fell with me.

We first heard of Woody when he was a five-year-old. 'Foxford' (the then Editor of *Horse and Hound*) had a great day on him with the Galway Blazers. And then my wife, searching for a horse for herself, saw him in Barbara Rich's famous yard at Thorpe Satchville, and told me that she thought that he would suit. I drove up to Leicestershire the next day. It was March, there were wisps of snow on the ground, but I just got there in time to ride him in the dusk. The first three steps out of the yard were enough: he arched his great neck, took the bit, and strode off purposefully, and has been more or less in charge of the partnership ever since.

When Woody was delivered, we had to make certain changes to our arrangements. As my wife was leading him in hand he jumped a gate whilst she was still busy opening it: he repeated the trick when a neighbour's horse happened to be passing. We had to re-fence much of our land, and, even now, if we are so unwise as to leave him unattended, he will hop over the paddock's iron railings, and come uninvited to the stable.

As a hunter he was perfection for about five seasons, then he suddenly stopped jumping. X-rays revealed navicular disease, the irreversible deterioration of a small but vital bone, acting both as a hinge and a pulley in the foot; it is the curse of large horses that have been over-used when immature, and a risk you take when you buy a horse of Woody's type and background. We have managed somehow, he and I, for the past few seasons, but soon the time must come when he enjoys the chase no more.

⁂ 1996 ⁂
FEBRUARY

How quickly the short lives of our boon companions speed by. If that seems too sombre a reflection for a February morning, read on: this chapter at least has a happy ending.

The thought came to me as, riding one old horse and leading another, I looked anxiously back to Perdita. Only yesterday, it seems, an inexhaustible puppy, today she is an elderly lady who cannot always manage the full two hours of exercise the horses need. My wife was to meet us halfway and drive Perdita home.

A favourite circuit climbs gradually out of the vale onto the downland escarpment, to where you may look down on a spot in which a pair of ravens are reliably said to nest. I always hope to see or maybe hear them, but never have. Ravens are believed to live to a great age, although none of my books confirm this. I know that they mate for life: perhaps this pair was there when I was born, or will outlive me.

Approaching the ride's highest point, where it winds through the defensive works of an ancient encampment, it was blowing a gale, and I again glanced back. Through driving rain I could make out Perdita, lagging in our wake and carrying what looked, for a nightmare moment, like the head of John the Baptist. I hurried on, warning her mistress, as I passed our rendezvous, that she had a present coming to her.

Next morning, while rearranging Woody's bed, I found the body of a pheasant concealed in the heaped wood-shavings in a corner of his box. Perdita, who had been nervously watching, transferred it swiftly to the kitchen garden.

In the failing light that evening, after hunting, she was trotting down the drive with it, now a Red Indian war bonnet, in the direction of the dung heap. At breakfast time, it was an empty pile of feathers on the kitchen floor.

Although once common enough, it is now rare to be benighted when hunting, thanks to horseboxes. But it happened, just before Christmas, when the Wilton hounds were with us, that it was all but dark when the visiting huntsman reluctantly blew for home. In the middle of nowhere, five miles or more separated us from the barn where both hunts were to share tea.

The small cavalcade – a pack of hounds and seven horses – headed west, following tracks much older than any metalled road. A moon was due, but not for some hours. The darkness was intense, only wisps of snow in the ruts and ditches, reflecting meagre starlight, betrayed the ground beneath our horses' feet, and we had just the rumps of the paler hounds ahead to give direction.

The huntsman occasionally blew, for the benefit of stragglers, and the rookery in Doles Wood was a-chatter as we passed – whether in our honour, or following their usual lights-out routine I do not know. Otherwise, only the horses' tread and the occasional admonition of a hound broke the silence. It was a time for thinking and remembering.

Both hounds and horses could evidently see well enough; certainly Woody never stumbled. But if the word came back 'gate please', and one was delayed, fumbling blindly with a fastening, he would panic to be with the others, and plunge alarmingly. At one stage, from just such a cause, a horse with an empty saddle joined us, but no harm was done.

We were grateful to be met by the terrier man with a lantern as we descended steeply to and crossed the only road. 'Escort to the Colours,' intoned the young MFH beside me – an echo from the parade ground that somehow exactly caught the flavour of the moment.

In a more modern mode, he had shortly before lent me his telephone to call my wife, to tell her that we would be home for supper. What I did not tell her until Woody was rugged-up snug, was that he had carried me so well, and through so long a day, that I could not bear to follow through our recent agonised decision that this was to be his final season. I cannot face parting with him yet.

APRIL

Many hands make light work, or so Nanny used to say, but, as with so much of the old nursery rubric, I often find the exact opposite to be equally true.

When I am working in the stables, 'Can I help?' usually means 'Can I come and talk to you?' and one has the choice of either pretending to hear what is only half heard, with all the risks that that entails, or of pausing while everything is spoken, as it were, in block capitals across the yard, or down the drive to the distant midden. Worse than that, the implement one needs is always in the helper's hands, usually as a prelude to being hidden. The upshot is that a chore which usually takes a twinkling lasts an age, and then often has to be redone, properly.

By the same token, foxhunters know the perils of joining a hunt other than at the meet. A few seasons ago, my wife and I went to look for hounds after I had spent a morning in the office. We came on them suddenly and from a wrong direction and received a well-deserved and public blasting from that demi-god, the huntsman. A case of 'better never than late' would you say?

Having, anyway, come late in life to fastening my affections on a dog, I am still discovering how much we humans gain from the give and take of close companionship with animals. I learnt to ride from my father as a rather nervous boy; but I learnt to love riding as a young man, from a horse.

That was the first of half a dozen free-going, bold, skilful, optimistic friends whom I have been lucky enough to get my hands on over the years. The latest in the line, and the best of them all, is in my stable now: he gave me renewed delight and confidence in riding to hounds, and I owe to him my emergence, such as it has been, as a hunting correspondent.

His heir apparent, Dandy, who since New Year's Day has been officially five years old, but is yet two months short of his real birthday, has been a joy; but we have taken his education as far as we are able, and soon he has to go away to finishing school to be taught professionally how to jump, and to learn how to deport himself in company.

I never dreamt what pleasure there was to be had in bringing on a young-ster. The farouche and unintentionally dangerous colt (what more accu-rately descriptive word is there in our language than horseplay?) has become a biddable, lovable and, when handled firmly, quite gentle creature.

No doubt my unpolished ways in the saddle have taught him bad habits, but I am confident that we will suit each other, which is all that matters, and he has surely educated me. He has taught me to believe that some horses, if not all, only need to understand your wishes to obey them: riding is essentially a language problem.

Like his mother, Dandy has one sock, which is a bit of a bugbear in a wet country, not, directly, because of the bore of cleaning it, but because paler skin seems to be especially susceptible to mud-fever, a potentially debilitating skin condition which is prevalent in the Dorset vale. I read somewhere recently that the entire London cab force was nearly grounded by mud-fever in 1871.

Dandy's sock became infected before Christmas, and my wife has been nursing it through this wet season. We try to keep him off the mud, and occasionally bring him in at night to let it dry thoroughly. However rewarding, keeping horses is a form of mutual servitude: while hosing Dandy's fetlocks, and picking out his feet, it tickled me to think that you might be reading this on Maundy Thursday.

MAY

Almost 200 years ago the poet William Barnes was born, if not just across the fields from here, only a couple of parishes away: he must have been one of the most gifted men ever to have come out of this vale. The son of a poor tenant farmer, with little education, he became a schoolmaster and devoted parish priest, and, although he left these shores only once, briefly, for a weekend in Dieppe, he achieved a working knowledge of 72 languages.

But the language that he chose to write in, and which he loved best, was a 73rd, the Dorset dialect, as spoken in the few square miles that stretch away north from this house, the Blackmore Vale. I have little taste for poetry, but his *Selected Poems* is one of two books that have for years sat alone on the table by my easy chair, the other is the poetry of his disciple Thomas Hardy.

Barnes grew up during the farming boom of the Napoleonic wars, and reached manhood in the depression that came with peace and renewed continental imports. It was a time when the screw was turned on poor agricultural families by the enclosure of the common land that they largely depended on for subsistence and any pretence to independence.

They must have felt helplessly at the mercy of distant, unknowing forces. The notorious 'Captain Swing' had his day. Rick-burning and machine-smashing were rife, and there was rioting throughout southern England. Round here, this ended when the militia dispersed insurgent labourers on a place above this house (I am looking at it now) which we call Dungeon, and is also known as Castle Hill.

The poetry I write of is very varied in subject. I prefer it when Barnes is describing the small change of village life, as in this lovers' tiff between John and Fanny which begins: "I thought you mid be out wi' Jemmy Bleäke.' 'An; why be out wi' him, vor goodness' seäke?" And ends: "But 'twull be over now, vor you shan't zee me/Out wi' ye noo mwore, to pick a quarrel wi' me". One should not take Fanny's punch-line at face value: reading the whole poem, you can almost hear wedding bells ringing out from St Mary's, Sturminster Newton.

JUNE

Since recently attending a course on bird-calls and songs at Flatford Mill in Suffolk, it is as if a new range of colours had been added to a familiar landscape. When I was out riding Dandy this morning, a now unmistakable nightingale disentangled itself from the ensemble playing in the depths of Broad Alders Wood as we went by; a few weeks ago he would have been just part of the orchestra. Nor would I have known before that it was necessarily a cock bird singing, such was my ignorance – robins are about the only species, I learn, in which the hen bird also sings.

The drumming of the greater, and much rarer lesser, spotted woodpecker is their song, and nothing whatever to do with foraging for food as I had always thought. It is its way of claiming territory, and advertising for a mate. The yaffle, or green woodpecker, rarely drums, and its familiar and often otiose or downright misleading cry of 'Wet! Wet! Wet!' is a call, not its song; in other words it is part of its everyday language, not a serenade or challenge.

I was recently watching one at a distance of less than 10ft, through a window. It was helping itself to ants down the side of the cover on the kitchen drain, peck-gobble, peck-gobble, elevating its beak, and giving a perceptible gulp as the wretched ants went on their last journey. I found myself wondering how it located an ant so unerringly, and then remembered. Coiled up in its head is the best part of a foot of sharkskin bootlace, its remarkable barb-surfaced tongue, anchored rather oddly, so my book tells me, 'close to its right nostril'. It throws this down, like a bucket down a well: it's quite simple really.

As I leave the house each morning the first sound I usually hear is a woodpigeon, Dr Proudie-like, soothing its wife: 'It's too true my dear, too true' and so on; then scatterbrained starlings on the stable roof whistle whatever comes into their silly heads and sparrows chatter from the front doors of their 'semis' by the rain-gutter. If the air is still, I can normally pick up buzzards mewing from Dungeon Hill before I leave the yard, and it would be a rare morning on which a blackbird was not making itself heard from the orchard. One nested on my rakes and hoes this year, rendering me 'excused gardening' for a month.

In the evening, the cock chaffinches are much in evidence. We have lots of them, and they are usually busy reminding the world of who owns what territory, before the sun goes down. For so small a bird they have a powerful song, and I have always found it pleasing. But now, walking round as light fails, I can pick out several other individuals among the background twitter, and make a reasonable shot at putting names to them. I suppose that we have about another month of birdsong left before the moult, but, thanks to Flatford Mill, the spring and early summer in Dorset will never be the same again.

It is exactly five years since my debut on this page, when, after a sleepless night, I dashed to Sherborne to see my first article in print. In those days a photograph accompanied the text, and there was our mare Daisy with her foal Dandelion for the world to wonder at, and Perdita, the stray who had recently joined us, making her first public bow.

We still have all the same animals, here or hereabouts, and Dandy has a sister, Bluebell. Daisy has been staying with a friend in Somerset for a year or so, hunting with the Cotley, but returns this winter.

Some readers will know what I mean when I say that, at the age of 23, she will still do for a South Dorset Thursday. People used to say that it was comforting to see her businesslike backside bustling over pokey places in front of them. She was incredibly competent, as well as sound, and I look forward to offering this service to her hunting friends again next season.

Of all the family, Perdie is perhaps showing her age the most. At bedtime tonight, when she gets up from her beanbag in the drawing-room to go to the kitchen, for nearly the two thousandth time, she will make funny little mincing, painful-looking, sewing-machine steps behind, which worry us. But she will fly the gate tomorrow when she comes out with me to see the horses – the question is, should I let her, and can I deny myself the pleasure of seeing her do it?

When I got home that morning in 1991 the telephone was ringing: I ran into the house to answer it. A local lurcher owner, a stranger, was calling to talk about Perdie, having just read about her. Putting the handset down, I expected it to ring again immediately, and perhaps go on ringing all my life: in fact, it has not rung, in that way, from that day to this.

Why does one write? Ask a robin why it sings.

AUGUST

Haymaking has been chaotic this year, there just have not been enough sunny days strung together. As I write, fields are still being mown which must be well past their 'best before' date, with half the crop's goodness wasted in the dropping seed.

We were comparatively lucky. Ours was cut in June when the weather looked set and perfect. But then a great tea cosy of cloud moved in off the Channel; there was torrential rain, followed by two muggy, sunless days – we despaired. Fortunately, most of the crop lay unturned, just where it had been cut, and it dried quickly when the weather changed.

Returning late on a Sunday evening from Smith's Lawn, I found my neighbour busy baling, and there was nothing for it but to get in at least one load. And, having got it home, for a quite different reason, there was no choice but to stack it.

Last summer, wasps nested in the old bales that form the permanent flooring of one bay of the open cowshed where we store most of the winter's supply of hay – this year, bees seemed to have taken their cue from the wasps. I am told that bumble-bees do not sting, but we all know, from recent experience with BSE, how difficult it is to prove a negative. I did not trust those great stripy, furry, busy, cross-seeming, buzzing things, and I had determined that that bay would be stacked after their bedtime.

Shifting 80 bales, twice, single-handed, is quite a job. My wife, who had halved the labour of picking-up by driving the horsebox as I loaded it, kindly visited me at intervals – to check that I was leaving a free exit for the bees. But I shall not soon forget the labour of lifting the last dozen bales into place, a form of reverse obstetrics; the furious sound of bottled-up rage and vengeance from the bees, who, sting or no sting, could not risk the cool air and darkness to harass me; or the constant nagging thought that the Editor of *Country Life* required an account of the polo I had watched at Windsor to be on his desk by breakfast time the following morning.

We had a great to-do loading the four-year-old Bella into the horse-box. She was to go to school: I cannot cope with her and her brother, and the old horse Woody, as we start to get ready for the hunting season. A rehearsal seemed sensible, even though her brother had gone in without demur, so I parked the box by a grass mound, where the ramp might not appear too steep, and to provide a soft surface to fall on should there be dramatics. This was just as well, as her first trick was to kneel down at the foot of the ramp, as if in prayer.

My experience is that any horse, however reluctant, will load, if you are sufficiently patient. A lot of carrot, and, depending on the temperament of the horse, a little stick, works, as a rule. But Bella was to prove the exception. We had started in the early afternoon, and when it was time to change to go out to dinner we were the same statuesque group: Woody loaded, to set an example; me at the top of the ramp holding Bella's leading-rope and a bucket of feed; her at its foot or, at best, halfway up. There was no option but to give in and make a better plan for another day.

The better plan was to take her to the local stud, her father's home, where there is a walled ramp, which acts rather like blinkers, and experienced help. Largely thanks to the latter, she loaded in half an hour, my kind neighbour lifting each of her four suspicious feet in turn, several times, until she was in. Then it was a case of: 'Quickly, up with the ramp,' and away we went.

SEPTEMBER

With the equinox only four days off, one must write of the summer as being in the past, but what a summer it has been. Here in Dorset my wife and I think of it as the most lovely we can remember, so temperate, the air nearly always moving, just enough rain and so full of colour.

If this year's was the first spring in which I really appreciated birdsong, by the same token this was the first summer in which I truly noticed the countryside fall silent in July and August. The absence of the gorgeous din that filled the local woods when I rode by, earlier in the season, is truly striking.

Now, looking into the heart of Broad Alders wood over a familiar gateway, and seeing the sunbeams strike through the tall trees, I am reminded of a church, empty and abandoned, its morning and evening offices, its prime and compline, suddenly left off. It is a hackneyed simile, but I know none better. However, the medieval masons were surely copying the ancient forest, so to say that great woods are like cathedrals must be to place the cart before the horse.

Almost the last to pack up their music were the greenfinches. Well into August you could not leave the house without hearing that descending skid of notes, like a child running its hand down part of a piano keyboard. Now the finches are starting to collect in promiscuous gangs about the fields, raiding the seedheads, the cock greenfinch betrayed by the brilliant yellow in his wing.

Only the robin goes on singing. As I write, I fancy I can still hear his bel canto, greeting me from the top of our oldest yew tree as I came home from evensong last Sunday.

But when the birds left off beguiling us, the butterflies took over. My eldest son, who knows his lepidoptera, took us to walk on Lulworth Ranges one weekend. We saw marbled whites, dark green fritillaries, gatekeepers, small heaths, small skippers, common blues, and more wild flowers than you would thank me for naming – the wild thyme, with its fragrance and its Shakespearean echo, lingers most fondly in my memory.

He also showed us what I had never seen before: the fossil forest, great bowls of what must have been massive palm trees. You could almost hear pterodactyls screech – who needs *Jurassic Park*?

One Sunday morning, after matins, the rector stood in his billowing surplice at the church door amid a cloud of painted ladies. My old horse, Woody, sometimes had a halo of red admirals, peacocks or tortoiseshells about his head as we plodded a downland track, flanked by rosebay willowherb. A brimstone, with its delicately pointed wings, was working the flower-beds as I stepped out of the house one afternoon, and, in the same glance, I took in the crimson, green and yellow of the yaffle that has haunted the garden the whole year through. Truly, this has been a Joseph-coated summer.

OCTOBER

We were recently at a country wedding, in a small, baroque, Catholic church of quite astounding beauty in the foothills of the Austrian Alps. Although there was nothing to show of it on the morning after, the previous evening had seen the first snow of approaching winter. Musicians and choristers had been imported from Vienna, and they performed, and we took part in, a Schubert Mass.

I find it difficult to say what most impressed me: the beauty of the bride, wearing her sister's wedding dress, as she entered on her father's arm; the strong feeling of family; the service, in three languages, our own rector generously allowed a part; the splendour of the church interior, the flowers, the music.

But really, thinking back, and to adapt Samuel Johnson's phrase, what most penetrated me was the piety of the congregation and their familiarity with the liturgy – there was no printed order of service. My enduring memory is of seeing a fashionably dressed young woman kneeling in prayer on the bare stone flags; it makes me feel ashamed to recall the levity of some English wedding congregations, and sad to think of what our own, so knowing, more modern society has thrown away.

The reception was at the bride's parents' nearby hunting lodge, and the family and Austrian guests were mostly in national dress, the women in dirndls and the men in loden. This also was a brilliant occasion, and the best of it was that there were no speeches. If you get asked to an Austrian wedding, my advice is: go.

To make a holiday of it, we also had a long-wished-for stay in Prague. If there is a lovelier European city than the capital of Bohemia I would like to see it. The unrestrained flamboyance of the architecture, reflecting the great confidence of an earlier age, has now been brought to life again in the recently repainted, many-coloured houses. That, next to the grandeur of the older, medieval buildings, and the history of the place (remember the Winter Queen, sister to our own martyred Charles I?) make the city a joy to walk in. There is a feeling of new freedom, art and music everywhere, and prices, although rising, are still amazingly low. Prague's new Renaissance is a thing not to be missed: but you need to hurry – when we were there so also was the pop star Michael Jackson.

'Has your husband still got that clapped-out old horse?' a distinguished *Country Life* contributor and ex-Cabinet minister kindly asked my wife, on first meeting her last week. The answer was a definite 'Yes'. Like Dame Nellie Melba, Woody is embarking on yet another final season.

On the day following the *Country Life* team chase he was painfully lame, the worst ever, and not on his sorry foot. We took his shoes off and had him X-rayed, expecting to find navicular disease in his hitherto sound near fore. What we discovered was a half-inch blackthorn concealed in its coronet (the bit where hoof stops and horse starts). We have kept him in regular light work all summer, the kindest thing for an old horse, and he is shaping up splendidly for the opening meet – in two days' time.

Today, as we started on our usual two-hour exercise, I could hear weird cries coming from a wood half a mile distant. It could just have been a buzzard, but a trapped dog seemed more likely, but no one sets traps round here.

As we drew closer, and Woody began to become seriously alarmed and reluctant to proceed, I knew what we should find. Distressed deer make an unbelievable rumpus, heart-breaking to hear. One of this year's fawns, half grown now, had caught itself in a wire fence and was calling desperately for its mother.

It is difficult to explain on paper just how neatly it had trapped itself. One strand of wire was caught under its groin, and another, lower strand was sawing at its hamstrings. Had I had ready access to a gun I could, and would, have immediately dispatched the poor creature – that would have been the kindest thing to have done. As it was, I freed it, and it scampered off, ungratefully, but moving reassuringly well. We resumed our way, stopping briefly at a water trough, so that I could wash my bloodied hands.

That was not the end of our adventures. When we were climbing onto the downland, we found that a farmer was 'tenting' his sheep on the path, that is to say temporarily grazing them in the public way. An old gate proved easy enough to pull aside, and to replace, but beyond that there was a flight of metal hurdles: thinking of the quondam Minister of Education, I gave a squeeze to the 'clapped-out' horse – he flew them.

DECEMBER

The theme of 'after the storm' has been so memorably evoked in children's literature that I hardly dare to venture on it. Who can forget how Alison Uttley (*Little Grey Rabbit*), or A.A. Milne described it, and where is Wise Owl going to live now that the giant oak is down? But I do not believe that as a child I was ever taken, in my mind, on horse-back among the wreckage of a gale, so here goes.

Horses reserve a special sort of idiocy for these circumstances. After no doubt a sleepless night, they come out of field or stable with tails lifted and nerves all a-jangle, their imaginations in overdrive, and immemorial instincts rampant. Monsters lurk in every gateway, and each rustling leaf is a ravening carnivore straining for the kill.

Even Woody, the most somnolent of hacks when there is no hunting in the offing, is for once delightfully lively: he shies constantly, and with a massive violence, enough one would suppose to topple a London bus should such an unlikely vehicle happen to be passing. And you may be sure that, in that event, he would quite happily throw us both under the bus's wheels rather than risk being savaged by a scuttling shrew, or by some sparrow twitching in the hedge.

After the mildest of mild autumns my cabbages are threadbare, there having been no early frost to kill the caterpillars, but, by the same token, many broadleaf trees were disastrously late in hauling down their canvas. Great limbs of oak strew Stonylongs, my neighbour's field, as we pick our way by the bridle-path to the road, which is also full of storm debris. When we gain the Ridgeway I find that an enormous ash is down, betraying the secure and secret world so long protected by its roots.

Woody duly bobs and weaves and jibs and snorts at all these manifestations of the world's determination to do for him - there is surely nothing in cre-ation quite so paranoid as a horse – but he at last settles down as we achieve the shelter of some Iron-Age earthworks, and start our long descent towards the vale and home.

My mind, gone scribbling as is its wont, thinking of this very page in fact, is suddenly recalled by the croaking of a raven. The great bird, for the moment allowing itself to be mobbed, as I watch, without warning turns itself from a freight plane into a MiG, folds its wings and drops like a falcon on one of its tormentors, dismisses the other with a flick of its 'frumious' bill, leisurely flies to the top of a Scots pine barely 50ft from me, and for ten full minutes sits croaking mastery and defiance.

Its great wings hunch at every croak; then for some reason it pauses, snaps off a handy twig, appears to play with it, then drops it, and goes on croaking. It is the best and most characteristic sighting of that spectacular, and, in these parts, rare bird that I have ever had.

My generation can just boast a pre-war infancy, and a wartime childhood: both provide precious memories. For most of the Second World War we were in a Devon that, looking back, seems incredibly primitive; with no electric lights, hand-milking, and horses involved in nearly all heavy work.

I used to accompany a farmer each morning after milking when he visited his traps – rabbits were staple diet, and a source of extra income. And a neighbouring shepherd once showed me a plover's nest, complete with its clutch of eggs, a magical image that is with me still.

The country was a wonderful place for children to grow up in, but my most enduring memories of that time are of a united people at war, and of the oratory of Winston Churchill. These things set standards against which it is not really fair to measure present times, but which we who can remember them cannot forget.

But stronger still are my memories of the even earlier days, of dawning consciousness in a world of servants, of nursery meals, rest after lunch and then a walk with Nanny, of learning to read from a governess, and to bed at six o'clock with a story.

Then it was that I first met Little Grey Rabbit (Christopher Robin and his friends came later, in an Anderson shelter) and picked up the notion of how thrilling an adventure it could be to get out among fallen trees and branches in gale-blown countryside.

How hard it must have been for my young parents and thousands like them, barely over the threshold of adulthood and just making a success of life together, when war came, to be so brutally uprooted, to have to quit it all; and to have to part, as it turned out for ever, with a familiar, comfortable world, and, for the duration, with each other. You might say that for them, and for us their children, the rest of life has been, in a sense, lived 'after the storm'.

❧ 1997 ❧
JANUARY

The great frost came down on us like a hammer just before Christmas, and, as I write, shows the first sign of lifting, nearly three weeks later. Something I never previously remember happened – the Christmas Eve meet with its tinsel-twisted manes and excited children was cancelled. We turned out as a duty on Boxing Day, knowing that there would be at least ten expectant people on foot for every mounted follower, and that the hounds could tow-row in nearby woodland without harming their feet on the needle-sharp open ground, but there was nothing one could safely do on horseback, and we were home by lunch-time. Since then it has just been a question of keeping our livestock fed and watered as best we can, and exercising the horses when and where possible.

With the frost, as usual, came the fieldfares from Scandinavia – an enormous foraging army of them, latter-day Vikings, behaving as though they owned the place. And lapwings, which we do not regularly see, favoured us with a visit from less-sheltered grounds. I love to watch them playing grand-mother's footsteps in the winter wheat, running a few paces, then freezing, then running again. If you disturb them they take off with an irritated squawk, and make their blunt-winged, graceful way to a safe distance, and start the game again.

Local species, who cannot better their conditions by merely shifting, seem to be bewildered by the severe weather, especially the bitter, cruel, desic-cating wind, and become surprisingly tame. My mother came face-to-face with a buzzard, sheltering like a beggar in the porch, when she went to lock the church, and we had a wren as an uninvited guest in our dining-room: how it got in is a mystery, down a chimney I suspect. It left, reluc-tantly, by the front door.

Thinking that I might get a rare sight of that shyest of birds, the kingfisher, Woody and I rode out into the vale this morning. It is like a delta here, and in a two-hour circuit we must have crossed a dozen or more hump-backed bridges where, with great luck, one may sometimes see a flash of azure lightning; but we had no such luck today. All the little streams that are usually busy-busy were completely still, like the whole of Dorset, clamped in a just perceptibly easing vice of frost.

FEBRUARY

'All right?' 'Yes please, we are running out of port.' So went the dialogue with the young man who hunts the hounds, at the conclusion of our recent meet. Although the field was only 60 strong – we never have big fields, thank goodness – the 20 visitors represented between them half a dozen different hunts. People come from far and wide to ride in the famous South Dorset Tuesday country, and it was the last vale meet of the season.

Hounds found immediately, just behind the house, in Great Wootton Wood, and away we went over Dungeon Hill, where some foot-followers told me they had just seen three and a half brace of foxes playing. Seven evidently healthy foxes, that was good news indeed, for mange, or 'marnge' as country people call it, has been moving into our area from the west. Pathetic stories abound of foxes, denuded of their fur and desperate for warmth. The man who shears for us told me of one he found curled up on the body of a dead ewe, borrowing the fleece to stave off its own inevitable death; and you hear of naked foxes who have burrowed in among bales of stacked hay. No doubt the recent frosts have given the quietus to many such poor starvelings.

My own part in what turned out to be a splendid day's hunting, which ended with two neighbouring packs unintentionally joining forces, was inglorious. I took the old horse onto the top of Dungeon, and, in good company it must be said, watched from that vantage point, knowing for sure that fox, hounds, huntsman and field would all process back to us in good time, like a captive ball returning to a child's racquet. The hill always seems to be a magnet to hunted foxes.

Then, after a quick bite at home, I took one of the youngsters for his first serious attempt at following hounds. He was as good as gold while things were quiet, taking an intelligent, well-mannered interest in the proceedings, and standing blissfully still. But, when the field set off at pace, he gave an unsettling buck followed by the clearest possible evidence that, like his mother, he was not to be held in a snaffle in the hunting field. I took him home: he hunts in a double bridle now.

APRIL

Alongside a large engraving of Flora Macdonald sheltering Bonny Prince Charlie in a cave or hovel after the Battle of Culloden, a coloured print – an oleograph, I think – of Sir Edwin Landseer's *Shoeing the Bay Mare* used to hang in our nursery.

I do not know what has happened to either picture. They are not in this house now, but they both, as it were, hang in my head. Parents, it seems, do well to consider carefully what images they expose their children to, and I was lucky.

I must have spent quite a proportion of my late childhood in blacksmiths' forges; we called them blacksmiths, not farriers, in those days. If it was not one of my father's horses that had to be taken over Giant's Head to Cerne Abbas, it would have been the skewbald pony I shared with my sister.

The forge had its distinctive noises, smells and images, and they linger in the memory, too. Most of all, I remember that the smith, although kindly, was not a person to be trifled with. With the quickness that a child has, I soon collected that the people who came with broken bits of farm implements for repair were in awe of him. They edged into the forge rather sheepishly, however urgent might be their errand, picking their moment carefully before interrupting, and courting him in their language, taking nothing for granted.

Then, one day when home on holidays, or on leave, I found that the system had completely changed. Horses were shod in your own yard. There were no more visits to the cavernous smithy, no fire of live coals, no enormous bellows, just a neat, mobile, gas-fired forge. Although I miss the old ambience, its smells and particularly the wonderful assortment of iron oddments that hung from cobwebbed rafters, it is an improvement beyond measure. No longer does one almost wear out a set of new shoes by merely returning from having them put on.

During recent years we have had a succession of farriers, all excellent, all friends. But we have never been better suited than we are now.

Our present farrier was, like me, a soldier for more than 30 years, and, although we served our time in two different regiments, they have recently, by a pleasant chance, been amalgamated. Therefore we are now, technically at least, old comrades of the same regiment. It is called the Light Dragoons.

Sergeant 'Duffy' Fox will not mind my naming him: we have just spent the morning together, I holding the heads, and he the resisting feet of our two youngsters. They still fight a bit, but he is incredibly patient, and hardy, as you must be to hang onto the foot of a lusty four-year-old who will throw his whole weight onto you, or kick, out of sheer devilry.

I do not know that there can be any more skilled manual job than to fit a shoe properly onto the hind foot of a young horse who is not yet resigned to the process. But the job was done, and, as always, done well.

Dandy, the older of the two, and the stronger, is a handsome bay. Time and again, while he is being shod, I am reminded of Landseer's image from my nursery.

JUNE

'Are you sure that you haven't bitten off more than you can chew?' 'Yes, absolutely.' Thus went the conversation over the breakfast table, typical of the marriage dialectic – female acuity sharpening itself on male evasiveness.

I was, in fact, not at all certain that it was a good plan to ride back from Yeovil, having delivered the horsebox for its annual health check. There were railways to be crossed, an unavoidable stretch of busy road to be endured, and a strange bridle-way to be threaded; but nothing would have made me confess to my doubts. I was determined on the adventure, such as it was, and was sure that it would do the young horse good, so off we duly trundled.

It is a question who was the more surprised; the clerk at the garage at the sight of a horse emerging from the lorry, or Dandy as he found himself in a busy yard full of goods vehicles, with the hellish din of morning traffic on one of the West Country's more lethal trunk routes thundering close by. However, we had only to sneak round the corner on a broad verge to achieve the safety of a minor road: in a minute or so we had quiet countryside to ourselves, the youngster convinced that we were going hunting, and striding out in the most delightful way.

Almost, but not quite, in Somerset, our lane suddenly dove into the dank seclusion of a narrow sandstone gorge, typical of that part of the Dorset border. After that, we got safely over the worst of the railways, the Waterloo to Penzance line, without the sudden irruption of a train as I was dreading (why did I not look at the timetable before leaving home?)

But as we subsequently crossed the River Yeo, a moorhen exploded from the bridge-arch below our feet, and half flew, half ran upstream in splashy panic, as moorhens will: Dandy obliged with a similar perform- ance. Dismounting, I put the lower strap on his grackle noseband – it was in my pocket. I had meant to make this adjustment to his brakes before we started, but had forgotten. It was to prove a morning of forgotten things.

We were completely in the country now, no houses and little traffic. A flock of strongly marked piebald sheep, a breed unknown to me, was grazing in a field beside us, and a girl crouched in the gateway by the road, feeding a lamb from a bottle. She clutched it to herself, stroking its throat to encourage it to suck. How I sympathised – there is nothing more anxious-making than a newborn creature that will not drink – but she smiled at me, her charge seeming to be intent on life.

Soon we were leaving the largest village on our route behind us, were past the worst of the road, over the last of the railway bridges, and nearly halfway home.

Our real troubles started when we left the road and at last struck out across what used to be, and is still called, a common, and which old surveys mark, with tussocks, as rough and undrained. In fact, it was enclosed and taken in hand some few generations back, but you can see why it was left so long in common ownership, and even today it retains something of the character of a wilderness.

The map – unfortunately still sitting on the breakfast table – had showed an almost straight path leading exactly where I wished to go. So indeed our path started, but we were brought up sharp by a narrow bridge, just wide enough to take a horse but not to turn in it, and with a wicket gate at either end. I leave it to you to imagine the complications of getting a green youngster over such an obstacle, leaving both gates secured.

This done, with a prayer of thanks that Dandy had not taken fright and broken his reins while temporarily tethered, we found ourselves in rough scrub, with no indication whatever of where our path onward lay. The few hoof-prints on the baked ground were enigmatic, the sun, my compass, suddenly withdrew its services, the country was close, there was no helpful sound to guide us, just a woodpecker's mocking cry. I began to feel bewitched as we blundered on.

Somehow eventually we got into fields. A line of open gates beguiled me, although I knew the direction must be wrong. After what seemed endless bafflement, we found a farmstead, a track and at last, a road. It was the same one that we had left to enter on the common an hour earlier: we were not a yard nearer home. Surrendering, I gave up the bridle-way and settled for a boring, often-driven road.

Dandy had been getting listless, but he perked up when we reached familiar ground; I dropped the reins and let him take me home. The whole journey was about 15 miles, I suppose, 'as hounds ran', and we were three hours at it. At lunch it was 'How did that go?' 'Oh, fine. Dandy behaved beautifully.'

JULY

It must have been about a century ago that this house was turned back-to-front by the arrival of lawn tennis. Writing in 1877, Mary Anne Evans (George Eliot), living then near Weybridge, recorded that a visitor 'brought an apparatus for Lawn Tennis... we played till we perspired freely'. She was to become mildly addicted to the new game. I revere the creator of Silas Marner second only to Jane Austen, but cannot think of that horse-faced polymath thundering round a tennis-court, without a smile, and without wondering what size she took in plimsolls.

I presume that it was at about the same time that the then rector of this parish had the carriage-sweep in front of the house turfed over. He was a family man: was it Cyril, who was 5ft 9.5in tall in 1886, or Eva, aged 15 in 1879, or Sybil, 14 the year before (twin sisters), who persuaded him that they could not live without a tennis-court? Their heights and ages, and those of many more, are recorded inside a window shutter in the bedroom below that in which I write.

It is a suggestive and a treasured record. One does not have to be super-imaginative to stand at that window, look through a pane of old, slightly distorted glass onto the turf below and hear the summer sounds of 100 years ago, and wonder what became of Cyril and his siblings. No one would think of playing tennis on our lawn today, there is not the room, and nine Georgian sash windows do not favour the modern game.

But vicarage lawn tennis was, as we all know, proverbially tame, as the survival of some of our original glazing shows.

So, thanks to lawn tennis, visitors to this house now come to a back door, threading a small courtyard, once the province of servants and tradesmen or the route of those with business in the stables. It is enclosed on two sides by the house and on the others by what used to be called offices – a small dairy or laundry with apple loft above, an open log shelter and a game larder. There is a pump in one corner which, almost in living memory, was worked daily by a small boy from the village, shifting water from the well below to attic tanks, for Eva's and Sybil's baths, no doubt.

It is a constant source of wonder to me how crafty small birds are. They will nest and rear young under your nose, and you know nothing of it until the leaves fall. They are then off wintering in the fields and hedges, or, maybe sunning themselves a continent or so away, planning to come and perform the same trick on you again the following summer.

This year, a pair of pied wagtails, for the first time any of us can remember, elected to nest in the log shelter in the kitchen yard. It was a crazy choice, with the constant comings and goings, human and canine: and until I put a finger into what I had assumed was an abandoned trial nest, on a brick ledge at the back, where you can reach but not see into, expecting to find it dry and empty, but encountering sundry small, warm bodies, I did not believe it was a serious attempt. The parents, forever delightfully busy on the flagstones, or commuting over the roof to the old tennis-court, deftly catching insects, seldom seemed to visit it.

Locally they are named Molly-wash-dish, but, rather than kitchen maids, wagtails remind me of little bachelor uncles, bobbing round at a wedding in their morning coats, proud of their starched linen, and kissing everyone in sight. In spring, there is no excuse for muddling their genders, you can easily tell who is who, the male has much more 'linen'.

Trinity Sunday brought a frantic fever of fly-catching and, at last, undisguised regular visits to the nest. And on Monday, it seemed at the time such a black Monday, I found two nestlings, briefly scrunched and left for dead by Perdita, when I went to collect a saddle from the stables. Both parents were crying imperatively from the stable roof: evidently it was meant to be a launch day. I rode off hoping, and, yes, praying, that they were calling to other, still surviving, young.

My wife later found one fledgling sitting hunched and helpless in the back porch. With a little help, it flew off, inexpertly, not to be seen again. But, during kitchen lunch, I saw the mother bird dart behind a flowerpot with a beak full of ravelled insects, and, wonder of wonders, come out, as it were, empty-handed. Sure enough, the fourth of her babes was crouching there, in dank sanctuary. We shut Perdie in the house, and on and off, I watched and waited.

At about half past three it emerged, walking as calm as you please, and looking quite grown-up, but in an Eton jacket rather than a full tailcoat. Out of the courtyard it went, past the stables, round the corner, under the horsebox and out of my ken, its parents in acrobatic chattering attendance.

DECEMBER

It is the same every month. At about the time that I look forward to coming in from the garden, or wherever, to put my feet up and read the less idiotic parts of the newspaper, I remember that it is the second Sunday of the month and I must get changed for Evensong. A struggle ensues, but Evensong always wins.

We are extraordinarily lucky in this tiny village to have a service every Sunday: all except one, which I do not attend, is from the old prayer book. It grieves me to the heart that the church hierarchy seems hell-bent – and I use the term advisedly – on depriving the young of their birthright, Cranmer's English. I will play no part in forwarding such crass wickedness. But otherwise, unless I am away from home, I try never to miss church on Sundays, and the service that I love best is Evensong.

It has a special and different beauty at each season of the year. Coming out of church in summer to full-throated birdsong and walking home towards the lowering sun is unforgettable rich pleasure.

But to be in the church after dark, as one is in winter, especially at our carol service, imagining it as a coloured, musical lantern hanging in the middle of the fields, or to be there when a sudden rain squall strikes, roaring in from the south-west and the distant sea, is a precious time. It takes one back to childhood – and to well beyond – puts one in touch with the souls who worshipped there and who, without any doubt, thought the same thoughts and certainly repeated the same words through centuries past.

The great Duke of Marlborough must have sat in our church as a boy; his childhood home at Roundchimneys Farm is within the northern boundary of the parish. But he was a Johnny-come-lately compared to the de Glanville whose Hamstone effigy is a few paces from our pew, and whose family left its name upon the village.

Thomas Hardy, as a young architect, played some part in the church's restoration, at which time it was found that the sagging north wall of the nave rested not on masonry foundations but on a line of coffins. One can picture him and his work-people, and the parishioners and rector scratching their heads at that.

I have always loved singing in church, always, that is, since the days I sang under the great Dr Douglas Fox at school. He was a one-armed musician, deprived of a virtuoso pianist's career by a wound received in the First World War. I remember him as the most charismatic, admirable, inspiring teacher. It delights me to leave a reminder of him on this page, and to think that some small boy at Clifton may read it, as I first read bound copies of *Country Life* on wet Sunday afternoons in the library at school, and go and ask someone: 'Who was 'Douglas Fox?' and be told of that great-hearted, saintly lion of a man.

A fall shortly before the opening meet has forced me more than usually into the company of Perdita. My wife says, without a hint of jealousy, that I am besotted with her. We sit for hours in the cab of the horsebox while I submit to the indignity of having my green horse better ridden by a younger man.

Perdita combines elegance with strength, and, except with anything she is intent on killing, has the most lovely nature. My wife is right, I dote on her. Last Saturday, after I had fed Perdita the crumbs from the bottom of a digestive biscuits packet, which she wore momentarily on her nose like a gas mask, she suddenly spotted a little brown animal with a white bib hurdling the tussocks on the verge where we were parked, heading straight towards us. Was it a stoat or a weasel? Their colours are similar. Then it came to me: a nanny once told me that a weasel could thread a wedding ring. It is a useful exaggeration. The stoat passed, oblivious of us, under the lorry, and away about its own murderous business.

FEBRUARY

There is a place near here, aptly named Spring Grove, where a familiar lane – I suppose one must call it a road now – takes a last dip before finally climbing out of the Blackmore Vale onto the Dorset Heights. A small, neo-Georgian pumping station, built in 1936 for Sturminster Newton RDC – a reminder of the days when we had local government – and a thatched cob cottage, on one hand, face a pair of what were once estate cottages on the other. As boys, just after the Second World War, we used to visit the keeper there, go with him on his rounds and learn about his birds, dogs and ferrets and how to handle guns. Keeper, estate and shoot are gone now but the place looks much the same. It is usually alive with birds, and deer are never far away – Perdita must be kept close at heel. It is a lovely place, full of atmosphere and memories.

Riding there shortly before Christmas, I spotted a mysterious raptor perched by a telegraph pole. I saw it, as one often does, against the light, in silhouette only, getting its size and shape clearly, seeing it briefly also in flight but catching little idea as to its colour. Halfway in bulk between a kestrel and a buzzard, it certainly was not a sparrowhawk. What was it? Some readers may have guessed already but I went home puzzled and conned over my books. There seemed only one logical answer, and that unbelievable; I put it from my mind, said nothing of it. One does not like to get a name for seeing marvels.

The mystery resolved itself a few weeks later. We were dining with a friend, an accomplished amateur naturalist. He mentioned that he never visited a certain remote wood, well-known to all those locally who shoot or hunt, but he saw a peregrine. They bred on the coastal cliffs but ranged quite far inland, especially in winter, he told me. What I had caught a glimpse of that morning was probably as I had deduced but dared not believe, a wandering female peregrine falcon.

A day or so later, riding beyond Spring Grove up on the downland, I came across another novel sight, so shocking it fixed me to the spot. Barnes Lane is a grassy ancient way, once much travelled, now just a little-used farm track and bridle-path. It was on Tess's route when she made her desperate pilgrimage on foot from 'Flintcombe Ash' to

'Emminster' (Plush to Beaminster) one Sunday morning a century ago at this time of year. I ride there often. In summer it is aflame on both sides with rosebay willowherb. Butterflies love the place – often one rides almost in a cloud of painted ladies and red admirals. Someone had dumped an entire house clearance on the track: a massive heap, a ton or more of broken furniture, bric-a-brac and paper.

It took me some time to take in the enormity and to arrange my thoughts. My eye wandered over what was obviously the flotsam and jetsam of a life; loved things, worn by use, all with their tales to tell, all now pitilessly exposed, hideous in that precious place.

Hate, rage and compassion fought with each other: rage won. Returning on foot, I picked over the boxes of old photographs and papers, until I found a name and address, telephoned and learnt, as I had expected that 'Old Mrs X has died. We paid Mr Y £70 to remove her things for sale or disposal'.

I rang Y, received in short order three calls: one blustering; one conciliatory, a woman's voice audibly prompting in the background; and the last, from his wife, desperate, pathetic and apologetic. Picturing a string of children in rags, despite myself I felt remorseful. It was too late; all the details had already gone by fax to the County Council. Barnes Lane was clear the next time that I rode there.

'Deliver us from Yeovil' naughty children at the grammar school in Crewkerne used to say at morning prayers: I have it on the authority of a former pupil, my friend the rector. I repeated the mantra, threading that unlovely place in the horsebox, on the way to collecting our old mare Daisy from her temporary home of five years, out beyond Crewkerne, near Chard. The mother of our two 'youngsters', she has been staying with a friend. The friend is moving, so Daisy must live out her days with us: she is at least 25. When she joined our other two old hunters, both retired, they gave her, their former stable-mate, a savage welcome. As if to say 'We don't want girls here', they repelled her rather obvious advances, driving her out of the field shelter and away from the hay. I visited them all regularly from dusk into moonlight, a one-man Social Exclusion Unit, and went to bed reasonably reassured. At dawn they stood in a huddle, close together, three old friends in perfect amity.

MARCH

I hate playing god with animals. But when you take on responsibility for a dog, horse, or whatever, you overdraw on happiness. Sooner or later the day comes when the account has to be squared, the debt called in – it is as well to be mentally prepared. As anyone who read my last page may have guessed, our old mare, Daisy, did not last the winter.

One very cold morning late in January, when I was due to be hunting the best part of 100 miles away on Dartmoor, and was walking to the car, dressed to go, a kind call from the huntsman forestalled me. Contrary to forecast, the moor was frozen solid. There was no prospect whatever of hounds being taken out that day.

I had already visited the outside horses, and Daisy seemed unwilling to move. For some days, instead of coming for her meals, she had had to be escorted to the hayrack. I would walk out to wherever dawn or dusk found her say: 'Come on old girl,' and she would plod confidingly beside me to the shelter, where I would, if necessary, elbow in to make a space for her, and ensure that she got her share of grub.

But on that morning she just would not budge. I took hay to her, noting that she would probably need water to be taken out to her later. When I told my wife, we both shook our heads. There was no spare stable for her, and what was the point anyway of bringing her inside? We both knew that at last her time had come, and what needed to be done.

By chance, our own hounds were due to meet next door that same morning. I went on foot, meaning to speak to the kennel-huntsman. He is a small man, David, who rides short, and he was on an enormous grey – I found myself addressing the toe of his polished boot.

With the old-fashioned courtesy that is the proud badge of hunt service, and owes nothing to servility, he bent down and replied quietly to my query. 'Is it old Daisy? Yes, sir, bring her along tomorrow morning.' The die was cast.

There had been an item on the wireless on the previous day that had caught my interest, and caused some amusement. Scientists had ' discovered' that emotions are, after all, connected with the heart: in other words, something that had been known, and indeed celebrated, for millennia was now 'official' and we were all authorised to believe it.

I left that meet feeling desperate, with a palpable constriction in my chest. Drove to Yeovil, of all places, on the excuse of getting in a load of fodder, but in truth to be by myself, to come to terms with what had totally surprised me. When it came to the point, I could hardly bear to think of having Daisy shot.

I deprecate sentimentality over animals: it is the cause of so many of our present problems. But, through three-quarters of her life, and quite a slice of mine, Daisy and I had spent weeks, months, if you were to tot it up, in each other's exclusive company. However unintelligent in our terms, horses forget nothing, and give their trust discerningly: there was a bond between that shy, nervous mare and me, as witnessed by the way she would walk beside me to her hay. By the end of an unhappy morning, my head had explained more or less satisfactorily to my heart where duty lay.

So Daisy's last day came. She boxed easily, thinking, I have no doubt, that she was going hunting. We drove the 20 miles to the kennels, and I left her stabled between two hunt horses, alert, interested in her neighbours, and aware of the smell and occasional sound of hounds. David helped me put some borrowed clothing on her, careful not to meet my eye; I gave her a hug, scooped up our rug and headcollar, and ran for it.

JUNE

'I talk to the trees, but they don't listen' went the old song: exactly the reverse is true with me. Like most ex-soldiers, I have poor hearing; in my case it lost its edge to the waspish two-pounder guns that my regiment's Daimler armoured cars were equipped with when I first joined. The crack of the high-velocity round leaving that short barrel was like a violent slap on both ears. But, if I were to be entirely deaf, I think that I would miss more than any other sound that of the wind in trees, particularly after dark.

We used to have an enormous copper beech here, which reached across the lawn and almost touched the house. Even on the stillest night, even when leafless in winter, it had comforting things to say to sleepless children; in a gale it was heroic. I believe that, as a hybrid, it was not supposed to breed, but one autumn before it died it chanced, by some happy freak, to place a seedling in the vegetable garden. My mother had this professionally transplanted to the lawn: the new tree is nearly up to the roof-line now. A year or so ago it hosted the family of a mistle thrush, which I take to mark its coming of age, but it still does little more than whisper to us in the house at night.

Thomas Hardy made a great deal of the different voices of trees, and his ability to distinguish them. There is a lot of this in *The Woodlanders*, which has it locale in an adjacent parish, and in his poetry. I used to think this notion rather precious, a bit overdone, but have come to revise that view. Even I, riding by a copse on a breezy day, find that I can shut my eyes and make out something of the different languages of, say, spruce, holly and broadleaf.

But the prize for celebrating the poetry of trees must go to Keats, describing (in *Hyperion*) a breath of wind in summer woodland after dark. I wonder if you remember it: 'Tall oaks... dream all night without a stir, save but from one gradual solitary gust which comes upon the silence, and dies off, as if the ebbing air had but one wave.' Was there ever a better evocation of that precious, childhood sound, an old tree's darkling sigh?

When people ask me, as they sometimes do, which of our two young home-made horses I like best, I usually answer in the same sense as I reply to a similarly frequent question, 'Which of Jane Austen's novels is your favourite?' The answer is, the one I have just ridden or just read. The least perfect of the novels came with me on a recent trip to Hungary, so I am in love with *Sense and Sensibility* again.

Bella, the little mare, just six years old when you read this, was my ride this morning. In the road we chanced to meet her father, now largely retired, poor chap, 'teasing' mares over a field gate at the local stud. To my great relief, Bella and he almost totally ignored each other, illustrating a facet of horses' perceptions and relationships.

What do horses make of us humans? It is a jigsaw puzzle which tantalises me, and of which a piece just occasionally comes to hand, as on this last St Valentine's Day.

February 14 was a Saturday, you may recall. I woke to a splendid pillow bulletin: a house guest, arriving after my bedtime, had offered to act second-horseman, so I could for the first time hunt on both youngsters in a single day. Bella duly found me sometime between 1 and 2p.m., and we saw a couple of hours of uneventful, sunny, scentless hunting. Was there ever a drier February? We have never had our fields harrowed and rolled in that 'fill-dike' month before.

Spotting our house from the downland escarpment, I turned Bella's head and shamelessly left the hounds, meaning to potter the few miles home. We cantered in an inviting 100-acre field; my mind must have wandered, she must have shied or stumbled, and I hit the ground. ('Serve him right for leaving early and larking on the way home', many will be thinking.) I remember only getting to my feet, hanging by the elbows on a gate, seeing Bella disappear at full tilt round the knap in the centre of the enormous meadow, wondering what on earth would happen next... and nothing more.

When I regained consciousness we were well on our way home. My coat told me that we had been hunting, I soon picked up where we were and pieced the day together, backwards. A dream-like experience, it was like emerging from an anaesthetic, not unpleasant.

But it was fully a week before the really strange part of the story occurred to me. That little, empty-bellied mare, free in an ocean of lush grass, had evidently chosen to come back to me.

I believe I know the reason why. Since she was weaned, only three living creatures have meant security to Bella; her brother, my wife and me. To adapt a phrase from *Persuasion* (chapter XII), 'You may think whether she is dear to me.'

SEPTEMBER

A great ash stands on the boundary of our land, providing generous shade for the horses and their water trough, and reaching out over the road beyond the hedge. Like so many of the older, isolated trees that give character to the English landscape, it is a grown-out pollard and, like most such, it was pollarded for a particular purpose – in this case as a waymark.

Our old ash shows where a footpath crosses the public road and enters onto our land, one of many paths that radiate star-like from the church across the surrounding fields, and that in former times brought in worshippers from all corners of the parish. One can just hear a stranger being given directions. 'You must turn in, over the stile, onto the parson's meadow, by the great pollard, and you will shortly find the church ahead of you'.

Such trees owe not just their characteristic hydra shape, but also their longevity, to the fact that they were 'girt' in adolescence. Their trunks were cut through at about 10ft from the ground leaving a 'bolling' (long 'o') from which could sprout new growth safely out of reach of grazing cattle or of passing deer. This gave them a low centre of gravity: pollards can stand their ground in the worst of weathers.

Just as the growth from willow bollings is still regularly harvested in basket-making areas such as the Somerset Levels, in this dairy country our old pollards would have been visited by the woodman at intervals to take a crop of rails for fencing. No doubt this practice went on until the availability of cheap iron wire made wooden rails unnecessary.

Pollards are heaven for wildlife. Their upturned armpits collect seeds and rain; small, high, secret water-gardens of ferns and mosses thrive there; creatures of all sorts breed and live in them. With greater age the trunks often hollow out and, strangely, their health seems none the worse for that – then they can become blissful kingdoms of the imagination for children.

The 'Smoking Oak' near here, which stands alone, enormous, dropsical, with its great swollen bowl, is a descendant, if not survivor, of the ancient Blackmore Forest. It got its name this century when naughty village children lit a fire in its generous internal floor. No harm was done to the tree, but there are still smoke marks, chimney-like, inside.

You can see pollards of most broadleaf varieties almost anywhere, once you get the knack of recognising them. Instead of the tall, tapering trunk that is a tree's natural habit, they have a multiple fork, usually just out of reach. If they have been regularly cropped, the fork may be gnarled and complex, or if, like our ash, they have been left to grow, great arms, some fit to be trees in their own right, will have stretched upward and outward at every angle, competing with their siblings for the sun.

One expects to find old pollards in parks and pasture; at regular intervals on the edge of ancient woods; in hedgerows to mark the extent of property; at the junction of parish boundaries; or where a traveller might once have needed help to find his way.

OCTOBER

I HAVE been thinking about the part domesticated animals play in our lives, turning the stiff keys and oiling the hinges of social intercourse, effecting introductions, promoting dialogue. Perdita ineffably graceful, doe-eyed, gentle and clearly female, is a passe-partout. On the street children stretch out hands to her; when she enters a room adults react as though she were a winsome child in a party frock.

Horses often seem to have similar extended functions. Such is the effect of the latest colander-shaped British Standard crash-hat, that several of the young ladies who hunt with us would be indistinguishable to me, one from another, but for their familiar mounts.

For my part, it is endlessly brought home to me that for many people I am no more that a relic of a much-followed and now much-missed horse. 'Where is Woody?' they say to me. It is time that I answered that question on this page.

At the end of last season, when both Woody and his inseparable friend, The Bean, my wife's old hunter, had idled the whole winter through, off games and at grass, wrecking our pasture and imposing a Herculean daily chore humping bales of hay, we found ourselves face-to-face with the a question of what to do with them. Both were 'gone in the feet' (navicular disease), but comparatively young and well able to enjoy life. It was unthinkable either that they should be split up or that they should follow their old companion Daisy to the hunt kennels. But what on earth was the alternative?

Salvation came in the shape of a chance remark overheard in the hunting field and followed up. There is a herd of some 200 horses – I shall not tell you where, it is oversubscribed and the owners would not thank me – who live out comfortable lives, in barns in winter and otherwise at grass, giving monthly the blood that is an essential element in setting up human laboratory specimens for the health service.

We asked a lot of questions, fretted somewhat about the Dracula bit, satisfied ourselves, joined a queue and eventually trundled all the way up in the horsebox to what a Victorian novelist might have called Blankshire, almost speechless with sadness.

In the event it was such an impressive establishment, so welcoming, that the occasion reminded me of delivering my younger son to the Dragon School. He vanished, like a liberated trout disappearing with a flick of its tail into familiar waters, and with not so much as a glance back at his woebegone parents. Woody and The Bean seemed delighted with their new friends and surroundings, far more interested in the delicious silage on offer than in our maunderings. I am no actuary but, given a free run, it must be a question which of the two of us will live the longest, Woody or me.

Daily I find myself wondering more and more whether or not the metropolitan man, who rules us, has seen the cloud that hangs over the smaller farmer and, if he sees it, whether or not he cares.

We are all prisoners of our childhood: mine was spent on and amid Devonshire farms in wartime. Farmers were, and remain for me, people who lead a hard outdoor life producing food for their fellow islanders. They have virtue in my eyes, as do seamen.

A neighbour told me recently that farmers were no longer buying lime: they could not afford to. If you connect those two facts and extend the line, as we were taught to do in geometry at school, it takes you somewhere horrible to think of.

In Yeovil yesterday a boy was sitting begging on the pavement. It struck me that he was tidy and cleanly dressed, that he was for that reason more than usually pitiable. My pace slowed when I had passed him – I could not go home, I found, without learning something more about him. I went back and asked him for his story.

It was not what I had expected, nor was it edifying, it was in fact the same old, sad litany, familiar from my days working with drunks and druggies in Taunton. I left him with rather more than the usual tribute to his situation and to my own conscience.

The point of telling you all this is that, in the original *coup d'oeil*, I thought that he was the start of the nightmare that haunts me: a boy in from a farm to beg.

NOVEMBER

The new hunting season finds us enduring what, on the Derbyshire–Yorkshire borders, I have heard called a 'tottering time'; just about everything that could do, seems to be going wrong in the stables. With only myself hunting now, we are down to two horses, both young, one still very green. It is about as unsuitable a string for an OAP as you could imagine – as kind friends keep pointing out to me.

'Why don't you get yourself a sensible old cob?' they ask. The answer is that our two home-bred youngsters are like children to us, and both, in their different ways, show immense promise; we just have to bear with their teenage ways for the present. Better times are round the corner, if we can but get there.

Meanwhile, Dandy, who is really going well at last, got pneumonia, or something very like it, following horrendous weather on the day of an adjacent hunt's opening meet. He came home from gentle work distressed in his breathing and with a high temperature, is on antibiotics and off games and the vet is one again connected directly to my bank balance.

His younger sister, Bella, whom I had no intention of hunting myself, jumped me into an overhanging thorn bush and dumped me at the first fence on the occasion of our own, almost equally wet, opening day a week later. Dandy will no doubt recover, and Bella will grow up as her brother did, in more capable hands than mine. I shall try not to write about either of them again on this page until I have a happier tale to tell.

I doubt that I am alone in feeling I lost an old friend on All Fools' Day. I refer, of course, to the final demise, after a lingering illness, of the 'Home Service' – or Radio 4, as it was foolishly renamed in an earlier, if less disastrous, flurry of own-goals by the BBC.

It is no exaggeration to say that I feel bereaved. Since long before I had a 'study' at school, and was allowed my own wireless, I had learnt to look on the Home Service as the companion of my every day. Unconsciously no doubt, my routine over the years had become linked to congenial programmes: they were milestones in my day.

Most notable was the half hour between 6a.m. and 6.30 when, having fed the horses, I would enjoy a honeyed mug of tea and hear, in short order, the news headlines, the weather forecast, a résumé of the newspapers and, what was for me the best programme in the whole daily schedule: 'Farming Today'. This all has been swept away to give time to an already overblown, repetitive and therefore somewhat stale 'news' programme.

The half-hour before lunch was a natural time to break off work and be entertained; and so one did, and generally was. This slot has been given to another of Auntie's spoilt brats, a 'consumer' programme, that is, one catering to the modern obsession with material possessions and health and safety. It is called 'You and Yours', it is 'Them and Theirs' to me.

Bath time, at half past six, nearly always offered something at least tolerable, sometimes raising hoots of laughter. Now it seems to be given over to morons performing to a compliant claque. I have tried, but almost every evening's offerings, in its different way, I find impossible to listen to.

However, what irks me most, and what seems to me to typify the changes, is the affirmation of 'The Archers', which now infects the air-waves twice on Sundays, and the demotion of 'Farming Today'. The one weekday programme that genuinely spoke, in practical terms, to a rural audience has been shortened, shorn of its best presenters, and moved to the wrong side of 6a.m. Thus an ersatz rural soap, a metropolitan quisling, has bested the real thing.

The diminutive bagpiper, that I for a moment fancied I saw and heard skirling up the drive as I turned into the paddock on return from exercising the horses one recent morning, was, of course, no such thing. It was my wife giving an airing to her teething grandchild, and some much-needed and well-deserved respite to his mother.

The last few weeks have furnished many similar reminders of the essentially selfless saintliness of young motherhood: I find them a more congenial harbinger of Advent than unwanted mail-order catalogues, 'Jingle Bells' and tinsel.

⚘ 1999 ⚘
JANUARY

If I were to tell you that I have just been cleaning up the drive after Dobbin, you might get the wrong impression. Dobbin is the man who cuts our hedges, and has done for several years. In the early days I was shy of addressing him as though he were a cart-horse, but when I learnt that everyone, including his mother, did so, and that no one locally knew any other name for him, I followed suit.

Granted that modern hedge-cutting is an unlovely business, some of the men who do it are artists. They tiptoe round one's land in their gigantic tractors, managing the flail as if it were a feather duster. Dobbin is just such a one; like many tractor drivers, and as his name suggests, he is enormous, and as with so many giants, he is remarkably gentle of manner, and quietly spoken.

Lord Grey of Fallodon appropriated for his own purposes, borrowing it from Milton, the only word in the language that adequately describes the way birds impinge upon our lives, when he called one of his books *The Charm of Birds*. Birds flash sudden winning smiles at us when we least expect it, perhaps darting in and out of an otherwise drab day, leaving small ripples of wonder and enchantment. As with charming people, it is perhaps wise to remember that they do not in fact care a fig for us – but they do impart something of real value.

The other morning, coming home, just as I passed the stile that marks the boundary of our land, a collared dove fluttered into the road in front of us, almost under the horses' feet, manoeuvred acrobatically, under their noses, and almost under mine, flirting its plumage to best advantage, and then fluttered down immediately behind us, for whatever titbit it was that it had spotted on the tarmac. It was an artless performance that nevertheless imprinted on my mind the delicate colouring of a bird, a recent incomer that I am not especially fond of, and almost made me its friend.

Again, just today, taking the bridle-path across my neighbour's field, Stonylongs, a small flock of waterfowl divided ahead of us, two scuttling one way and three the other, where the meadow narrows into a droveway. They were moorhens, almost my favourite bird; this family breeds on a pond nearby, and defies the foxes by roosting rather inexpertly amongst the thorns and brambles in the hedge. Such busy, deedy, pretty little creatures, they have charmed me since childhood.

Perhaps my most memorable close encounter in recent years was with an exotic golden pheasant, nearly twice the normal size, with immensely long and striking barred tail feathers, which seemed to adopt my old horse Woody and me as we entered a nearby wood. It accompanied us, at heel, like a dog, stopping when we stopped, and then coming on again, for almost a mile. We left it clucking and chirruping most musically. I have often looked for it since and not seen it: too easy a target to survive that winter I suppose, but I shall never forget the rainbow moments of its company.

The other Dobbin who cropped up just before Christmas was of course in the televised version of *Vanity Fair*. William Dobbin has always been something of a favourite of mine, and it was irritating to find that, as so often, the casting director, or whoever, knowing better, chose to ignore the obvious prompt of Thackeray's choice of name for his character, and his precise description of him as 'a very tall ungainly gentleman, with large hands and feet, and large ears, set off by a closely cropped head of black hair'.

When I was myself an awkward young army officer I took Dobbin to heart as a *beau idéal*, wrote Thackeray's verdict on him on a scrap of paper, and carried it in my wallet wherever the Army took me, until it became illegible with wear. You may find the passage at the end of the one-but-last chapter of the book, 'all the poor, all the humble, all honest folks, all good men who knew him, loved that kind-hearted and simple gentleman.'

APRIL

'Try knit-bone' a friend suggested at the point-to-point, when I was in the fourth week of nursing a broken collar-bone. Chambers, never normally at a loss, did not acknowledge knit-bone, but the farrier, Duffy Fox, immediately recognised it as a name for comfrey, a common herbal remedy: the stuff grows in our paddock. He was right, as usual, the label on the bottle called it Symphytum, and the normally excellent dictionary could not be faulted twice.

Whether or not the comfrey made any difference I cannot tell. Almost exactly at the eight-week point, as the surgeon had predicted, I began to feel in one piece again, and could ride with comfort for more than half an hour, and think of hunting, if only to get down to Exmoor before the season closes.

Dandy, blameless partner in the fracture, has been taking a herbal remedy too. Following the advice of a neighbour he has been having garlic with his feeds, in an attempt to banish a lingering slight cough, such as many of us have been left with after this winter's devastating flu. Again, I have no idea whether or not the doses acted: he is not coughing now, but his stable and the feed-room smell like a French bordello – I believe.

Meanwhile, expertly ridden, he has added a further two team-chase rosettes to his tally. Born here, exactly eight years ago, he has turned into a topping horse. His sister Bella lags a bit in her development, and has gone for a spell at an expensive boarding school: he misses her, and so do I.

At a time when most of us are ruefully aware of increasing rates of local taxes, our County Council has chosen to litter the countryside with expensive looking signs showing where footpaths and bridle-ways leave roads. I use the word 'litter' advisedly, the signs are ugly, unwelcome artefacts, banners of officialdom, newly disfiguring many a favourite hedge. They are also unnecessary, duplicating, and in some cases triplicating, existing entirely adequate, discrete, robust and simple signs, small unambiguous arrowed discs fixed to gateposts.

But worst of all, they have been erected so hurriedly, 'in time for the millennium', that many are already standing drunkenly askew, pointing who knows where. I was able to measure the first one that actually fell down: the post, 7ft 9in long, had been sunk about 12, or at most 18in into soft vale clay. What sort of an idiot, one wonders, supposed that it would survive a gale, let alone the rough-and-tumble of cattle and farm traffic squeezing by?

It would be interesting to know the cost of these signs, and of their erection, and to calculate how many hours will be squandered on their maintenance, until the wretched things are either properly seated, or eventually taken down and disposed of. No doubt this baneful exercise in futile waste is being trumpeted in some daft committee as the glory of the age, whilst, with much hand-wringing, Dorset has decreed an increase of 7.9% on last year's punitive rate of tax.

Anyway, why must the authorities be forever putting up more signs? All are obtrusive, some are quite pointless. One thinks particularly of the myriad 'No footway' signs on roads where no one but a bureaucrat would expect to find a pavement. Recently we have been blessed with a rash of signs announcing 'Wildlife Verges' – how can a thing be 'wild' that has a sign on it? – and there is even talk of putting up 'poop scoop' signs in this tiny rural village, as though it were part of Bournemouth and we would go to war with our neighbours over a bit of dog dirt, inform on them, and get them fined £100, as the signs threaten.

To hell with signs I say. Let them be made to take down two for every new one they put up, or we shall soon have more signs than trees.

I have been admiring a copy of a picture by Charles James Adams (1859–1931) that I would much like to own. Called *Waiting to be Roughshod*, it shows a group of cart-horses in an evening light, outside a busy forge. The word roughshod, so often used in metaphor, intrigued me. I had not made the obvious connection with farriery: for the first time I thought to enquire what it exactly meant. Duffy for once was stumped; but Chambers gave the answer, it means 'provided with roughened horseshoes'. The clue was in the background of the picture, a deep frost.

MAY

'Alright if Brian does the harrowing now?' asked the voice on the telephone. 'Yes, of course, how kind of him' was the answer. What else could one say if a busy young farmer was prepared to turn out to do us such a favour on a sunny evening? How could one plead that a dozen guests were expected for dinner in half an hour; that I was not yet changed; that the young horses would need bringing in from no doubt the furthest corner of the five-acre field, where they seem to spend all their spare time gazing vacantly over the hedge into the road beyond (collecting car numbers I swear); that the sheep would need thinking of; that several gates must be tied back to admit the tractor; and that the jumps in the paddock must come down, with all their bits and pieces dragged out of harm's way?

'You've got five minutes' called my wife as I got back to the house, having seen the harrowing start. Blessing Sandhurst, where, if you picked up nothing else in that first chaotic junior term, you learnt how to change quickly, I crashed into the informal gear that we all seem to wear at dinner parties in Dorset these days, and presented myself for inspection, breathless but on time. The first of our guests arrived just as the first cork popped.

It takes, I learn, exactly as long to harrow six acres, as to get twelve people to the point of dining. Just before we went in, I and the best-shod guest put the horses out and shut the gates. It was dark: the wonderful birdsong, which I had sampled every time I had put my head out of doors to check on Brian's progress had ended, the last cock chaffinch even having folded up his music. The two horses, rather puzzled by it all, trotted off, hungry and grateful, into their strange-smelling field. Perhaps it is no bad thing to be rushed into a dinner party, I enjoyed the evening immensely.

We children, the four of us, had a favourite aunt and uncle. They were childless, lived in London, he a stockbroker, she the eldest but one of my mother's five sisters. They always came to us at Christmas, Matthew having his one day's hunting of the year on Boxing Day: what a stiff figure he must have cut after the holiday, on Throgmorton Street, and in the offices of Capel-Cure! My sister and I would hack the ten or a dozen miles to the meet, leading the grown-up's horses off our ponies. Those Christmases were a precious ritual, and are a precious memory: I find myself wondering if children have aunts and uncles like that now.

Born in 1893, my uncle was old enough for the trenches. I have a picture of him in a regimental group, a boyish subaltern, sitting cross-legged at the feet of the CO of the 6th Battalion of the Royal Scots Fusiliers, an unhappy-looking Winston Churchill. In the next war, too old for active service, he joined the RAF, and did something in a junior rank in the Air Ministry. But when, at about this time in 1940, the SOS went round, Matthew helped to crew some tub picking up our soldiers from the beaches at Dunkirk. My Aunt Margie, not Roedean's head girl for nothing, made herself useful in the WAAF.

They were a good-looking couple, glamour personified to us children, and their flat in London was a home-from-home, a base for our first tentative, inexpert sorties into metropolitan life. Neither of them learnt to drive a car: sailing was their passion. They kept an ocean racer at Lymington, commuting there by train. Our summer holidays would occasionally be punctuated by welcome summonses to join 'Driac' at such-and-such a place. Then we would cruise for a day in the Solent: which was when I picked up the very little that I know of sailing, including that, even in the lightest sea, I am nearly always sick.

On the morning following the 'harrowing' dinner party came our neighbour's wife, in her hand a fax from Canada. Would we help finally to decide a question busily debated in our circle this past year, the name for her husband's new yacht? When you read this, my wife and I will be on inland passage from Lake Eyre, via the Mohawk and Hudson Rivers, to Long Island Sound, the first leg of 'Quicksilver's' maiden voyage.

JULY

Since returning recently from New York I have been mentally comparing it with this small Dorset village: can they really both be on the same planet? One of the best views of Manhattan must be the one we had on the magic evening of arrival, from a mooring on the New Jersey side of the Hudson River. Thence one just had the impact of the familiar massive pile of buildings, with really no evidence that, on a working day, nearly 20 million people strive there. But that was not allowed to be enough, one had to go and touch the place: I am glad we did.

On the first visit, three of us climbed the Empire State Building, which is not to be missed, and is a good way to get the lie of the country. Then, whilst the womenfolk explored 5th Avenue, I walked north towards the greenery of Central Park, and later, almost the full length of 7th Avenue southwards, to the giant twin towers of the World Trade Centre, to catch a ferry back to our moored boat. I found the place entrancing. One could do without the smells and hellish noise, but the life of it all is as bewitching as it is bewildering, and the people, so heterogeneous, seemed universally kind.

On the day following, my wife and I walked in Central Park, a veritable playground, quite informal when compared with our London parks, and magnificently treed. After the grid-iron of the streets, it was very easy to get lost in the park, but we eventually found the Metropolitan Museum, and spent the rest of the day in that amazing treasure house.

It was there that, sorting through my small change on a table in the restaurant, trying to work out which confusing coin was which, I found amongst the dimes a silver 1836 William IV four-penny piece. Now how long do you suppose that coin has circulated in disguise, how and when did it cross the Atlantic, and was I really the first person in all those years to recognise it for what it truly was? You may be sure I did not put it back in circulation.

We were glad to return home, we always are, however unforgettable the interval. Perdita was beside herself to see my wife, literally crying with joy at the sudden ending of her supposed orphanhood: she seemed quite pleased also to see me.

All was well, inside and outside the house, except for the unwelcome attentions of two species, who seem especially to benefit from either the officiousness or the ineffectuality of modern government. Badgers, once such welcome visitors but now far too numerous, had made unprecedented excavations on the lawn – and thieves had returned. Having broken into the tack-room again, and found it empty, they cut two locks off an outside stable door, removing my 90-year-old mother's new lawnmower.

The police, as ever charming and prompt in their attendance, can apparently do nothing to deter this thieving: and the detective function, if ever it existed outside children's story-books, has atrophied. Here in rural Dorset we are robbed at will, sometimes in daylight, by people who seem careless of the risk of being caught red-handed, and need have no fear whatever of being prosecuted. I wish that our authorities might take a lesson from the Mayor of New York.

AUGUST

Summer or winter, weekends always seem to be the busiest of times. Events, each with its own imperative demand, each often wanting to monopolise the same bit of a busy day, tumble helter-skelter, one on top of another. Before you know where you are you have been pitchforked from the middle of one week almost into the middle of the next, with barely time enough to pick yourself up and get ready for the following weekend.

Our village held its church fête last Saturday. Bella, the youngest of our two horses, had to have a two-hour workout in the morning, preparatory to cross-country schooling on the following Monday. The sheep, grumbling all the way, had to be persuaded out of the paddock, past the attractions of the vegetable garden, into the orchard, so that the paddock could be turned into a car park, which then needed to be signed.

Spare broccoli plants had to be dug up, bundled in dozens, dunked in a stable bucket, and taken, with some young self-seeded Judas trees and other goodies, to various stall-holders in our neighbour's garden. And then, just when I thought I was abreast of things and that it was time to get changed in order to oversee the start of parking, the local garden centre rang to say that the leek plants, ordered and forgotten, were waiting to be collected, and, were, presumably, gasping for immediate attention.

At the fête I take the entry money: my wife helps with the teas. Restraining the waiting throng until the appointed moment of opening, usually 30 or 40 people, longing to have the first go at the bargains on offer, is perhaps the least comfortable half-hour of the year. But after that I sit, very happily, 'at the receipt of custom', taking 40 pence off neighbours and old friends, and our fête's habitueés, who bring their familiar nameless faces from all over Dorset every year.

Maybe the postman will come from Sherborne, a much loved figure whom we only ever see on this occasion in mufti and off-duty; and some of the Second World War evacuees will again make their annual pilgrimage to the scenes of childhood. Through it all Perdita lies, disapproving, in the shade of a bush behind me: she hates the fête as much as I enjoy it. She feigns sleep, ignoring compliments and blandishments alike, just occasionally swearing *sotto voce* at any dog that has the nerve to trespass on her ground.

Leaving my post earlier than I ought, I catch the garden centre before it closes, and plant out 60 baby leeks, puddling them well in against a Saharan weather forecast – leeks are very forgiving, and try harder than anything I know to survive transplanting. I unscramble the carpark, reluctantly we duck a cocktail party, I get my work ready for the morning, and we fall into bed.

Sunday meant 'best kit', the 100-mile drive to Cowdray Park, and the best lunch, and, as it turned out, the best polo match of the year. It was an unforgettable day, with 'the widow' much in evidence (we used to drink Veuve Clicquot at the slightest excuse in my regiment). But we arrived home to the disastrous discovery that *Sense and Sensibility* was just starting on TV, and were kept from bed until midnight by that delightful and ingenious film version of Jane Austen's only less-than-perfect novel.

Monday starts at the full gallop, with a copy deadline to be met by break-fast. The leeks, who did not enjoy Sunday, silently scream 'Water' as I leave the house to ride, and, before anything else is done, each must be individually requited, like a hungry nestling. Dandy cannot be left without exercise for another day; his sister has to be carted to distant Rockbourne, to be expertly schooled over the cross-country course there.

Meanwhile 'they', who must not on any account be put off, had come about the chimney (a full-grown tawny owl had somehow appeared in the drawing-room grate a short while ago). As even the best builders will, they had left the whole house upside down. Grass was clamouring to be cut, and there was a PCC meeting. Suddenly it was Tuesday.

SEPTEMBER

Dandy and I have been plodding round the parish delivering letters, 71 of them. I left out two households which I knew were 'anti', valued friends and neighbours both, and about half a dozen where I felt the occupants were too old, or were not well enough, to be vexed again with the old, tired squabble about hunting.

It was an interesting exercise, involving a first-ever study of the electoral roll and reminding one of how venerable the parish boundaries are, and how out-of-date. My object was to discover who might come on the next countryside march, whenever it should be, and who might be prepared to help with the empty-seeming chore of writing letters to MPs, with the demeaning business of telephoning votes for TV or radio debates, and so on.

Each call involved getting down, improvising some means of struggling to a letter-box, with Dandy at full stretch of rein, or left for a few breath-less seconds to his own mischievous devices. Always on the lookout for a snack, he would browse shamelessly among shrubs, flower tubs, or borders, and I would rush back to him and snatch guilty blooms from his champing jaws.   Four days it took with afternoons in-filling locally. Perdita my then reluctant colleague, unamused and disaffected, interested only in the endless examination of time-consuming smells. If only I could have explained to her that it was all in aid of 'hunting with dogs'.

Where were you when the lights went out? I suppose that everyone has an eclipse story: ours opened in farce but developed almost into tragedy. It must be some sort of recognised modern paradox that the more you hear and read about something, the less you take in. I had been so swamped by eclipse hype and guff that, by the morning in question, I had grasped two 'facts' only – that if I so much as peeped at the wretched thing I would go blind, and that, even here in Dorset, we would be in total darkness for some unspecified period. We needed to get the horses exercised and safely indoors I believed, so that they might not fall about and hurt themselves during the mid-day night: and I warned my nearest and dearest to keep their eyes averted throughout the whole dangerous phenomenon.

As we were walking the horses home, Bella suddenly fell on the uncertain surface of a newly-gritted road. My wife was unhurt, but the little mare took the skin off both knees, one very badly. It was a sight to break the heart: she looked like the Earl of Gloucester, or Oedipus, with two great bleeding eyes for knees as I led her home. I cannot remember feeling so heavy-hearted, since her mother did almost exactly the same thing ten years ago – there was some comfort in that thought anyway. Daisy had made a total recovery. Bella was in shock, shaking, and evidently in considerable pain when I got her to her stable, and we were beside ourselves to comfort her – flesh of our flesh almost, we had doted on her since the morning six years ago that she was born.

Hours later, it seemed, the vet arrived (in fact she was very prompt). 'Look!' she said, and, forgetting everything, I looked, and saw the sun, a cuticle of burnished silver through the cloud. I bustled to get the lorry out, drive Bella to the vet's hospital, and get her safely unloaded before darkness should double difficulty. It was only as I drove the empty horse-box home that I realised that the eclipse, and its bathetic shadow, had long ago passed over us: the lights never went out, and were never going to.

NOVEMBER

Even today there are still bits of *The Times* that are worth reading. Not being interested in footballers or fashion, I usually ignore the news pages and start my brief daily skip through this once revered newspaper from the back page, looking first of all for the obituaries, and never failing to read those of people who saw war service. Their lives speak of native grit and heroism, and connect with a history, some of which I lived through as a child, and of which, despite the current fashion for modernity at all costs, I remain unspeakably proud. Sometimes, someone who has lived quietly among us, almost forgotten, suddenly blazes into life as a hero on this page.

We used to have a saddler, who, with his wife, kept a shop in Cheap Street, in Sherborne. A small, quietly spoken man (he needed to be small, as you shall learn) it was not difficult to forget his rank, and who he was – which was just as well. Handing an admiral some insignificant, grotty bit of tack for repair 'as soon as possible please', would not otherwise have been easy.

At the age of 22, in the early hours of 22 September 1943, our future saddler, with one companion craft, sole survivors of the force of six under his command when they were cast off 150 miles from the Norwegian coast, took his midget submarine into Altenford. Against all the odds, exhaust split, compass useless, air supply running out, once entangled with a moored mine – which he detached 'by deft footwork' – and twice fouling protective nets, he placed his two tons of explosives to such effect that *Tirpitz*, the scourge of Arctic convoys, never saw the open sea again. She was finished off by the RAF the following year.

The Times of 30 December 1994, tells us:

> *At 8.12a.m. all the charges detonated, blowing X7 clear of the nets, but cracking her hull. He dived the boat to the bottom, to examine the damage, but had to bring her up again, with almost the last of his stored air. Riddled with fire from Tirpitz, X7 suddenly started sinking: Two of his crew were lost, but he and another were taken prisoner, and spent the rest of the war in captivity.*

Many readers will have realised that I am quoting from the obituary of Rear Admiral Godfrey Place, VC, CB, CVO, DSC. God rest his warrior soul, and those of the thousands like him, whom we especially remember at this time of year, as we poppy sellers go about our patches, and as this war-torn century closes.

How is Bella? Our neighbours ask: perhaps some of you also will remember that she fell and broke her knees on the day of the eclipse. When we got her home, after a fortnight in hospital, every day, twice a day for a month, we cleaned and dressed her several wounds, and put her through the demanding physio prescribed to keep her knee-joints mobile. She seemed to be doing well and was out at grass by day, when suddenly, on the leg with the worst wound, the infection got into the joint.

After more hospital and more operations we have her home again, strictly mewed up in her box now, just led out to graze, in hand, briefly twice a day. By a strange contradiction, this little firecracker of a chestnut, the brightest ride I have ever had, is a perfect patient, submitting trustingly to every horrible thing we have to do to her. We just have to follow the vet's instructions, and for the next fortnight keep our fingers crossed.

Birds are a constant source of interest and pleasure. Riding Dandy home one recent bright October morning, a group of three buzzards claimed attention. They appeared to be about some important, noisy business: 'This is our tree, go away!' two of them seemed to be saying to the third. After a bit, I realised what was going on. Transformed at last from a treasured egg into an unwanted gooseberry, a young bird was being told by its parents to go out into the wide world, find its own territory, and, as children's stories used to say, seek its fortune.

DECEMBER

On another day and at a different time, it could possibly have been the sound of a hunting horn that struck my ear as I left the house for the stables early one recent morning. The same noise, coming from the direction of the Manor House, kept cropping up occasionally thereafter, each time to be briefly puzzled over and again forgotten. Evidently it was a cow not completely happy in its situation; no doubt all was in order, someone responsible must have the matter in hand.

The mystery resolved itself when a young neighbour approached me, walking our boundary, on the following morning. One of his heifers had jumped out of its field, crossed a road and jumped into the home meadows of the Manor House. The problem was how to get it out. We discussed various unlikely methods of enticing her across the fence. His parting words were 'She's as regular as clockwork: she'll be bulling in a few days time, and will certainly jump out again'.

That afternoon, a 'woof' from Perdita drew attention to a black face among the brambles in the hedge that overlooks the stable yard. Staring at me, and seeming almost to be contemplating a Badminton-like leap across the Squire's boundary ditch for further discussions with Perdie, she looked a sporting little creature. As I brought the horses in together, they both managed a stagy start at this Cheshire cat-like apparition, before deciding that their tea was more important. It is the sort of theatricality that you can do without when you have a large horse in either hand. What with one thing and another we were all becoming aware of this unruly, vocal and unsanctioned neighbour.

Cattle recurred in my thoughts on the following morning when riding Dandy into the next parish to collect the horse-box from the garage. Our route took us along an old drove-way, one of the few that I know of that is still, for a short distance, almost perfectly preserved. A white nanny goat appeared in the crown of the bank on our right, it had evidently gnawed through its tether. Dandy obliged with another splendidly histrionic stagger: the goat chewed on phlegmatically. I could see its owners, travellers, encamped in the field beyond – they lay the drove hedges, and do it beautifully.

Droving, in its season, must have been an all-engrossing feature of local life through medieval times, right up until the practice was killed off by railways. Like travel by stagecoach, it died almost overnight: but, lacking the romance of the road, cattle-droving, the province of unlettered people, has left us virtually nothing by way of art and literature. We just have to guess what it was like when these broad grassy ways were full of great herds of lowing cattle, grazing as they went, in our case moving eastward to the larger market towns from the grasslands where they had been reared.

Drovers themselves will have been tough, itinerant people. Surtees gives us an idea of the type in his final Jorrocks book, *Hillingdon Hall*. The hero, grocer now turned squire, has retired to County Durham, but is by chance reunited with his old huntsman, James Pigg, who comes droving 'scotch kyloes' down from his native Borders. Kyloes, Chambers tell us, were the 'small long-haired cattle of the Highlands and Hebrides', and 'Hillingdon Hall' was in fact the author's own Hamsterley Hall; you can see the drove-way on the local map today. Those particular chapters are among some of the best that Surtees wrote, as well as containing the only reference to droving that I have ever come across in literature.

What we may be sure of is that those who owned land adjacent to drove-ways made good their fences, as you may still see today. I do not doubt that they locked up their daughters too.

⁂ 2000 ⁂
FEBRUARY

'Don't worry, darling, there will probably be no one there who knows any more than you do about the subject.' This wifely attempt to boost my self-confidence was patently unlikely to be true. Foolishly flattered by the invitation, I had agreed, more than a year before, to give a lecture to a local society at The County Museum. The then small cloud on the horizon, as small clouds will, had for weeks now covered my whole sky. I was petrified – it felt worse almost than getting ready for a point-to-point.

With an hour to go, we were changing. Colour-blind as ever, I had put on the wrong suit, a five pound note in its ticket pocket reminding me that there had been no collection at the last funeral it had been to. An absurd belief that it is bad luck to correct dressing errors made me hesitate, but I could not go in a black suit. I changed a second time, feeling more and more that the whole enterprise was damned.

Just how bad the lecture was I may never know – people are too kind to say – but it felt terrible. I might have bolted in the interval, had my wife not been there to steady me. A kind member of the audience at that stage showed me how to focus the slides, with a toggle on the gadget in my hand (you would not suppose that I had once commanded a regiment of tanks), and things perhaps went slightly better. I left the place swearing that under no consideration would I ever agree to give a lecture again: but an offer to ride one's special hobby-horse is so beguiling, I dare say that, given the chance, I shall fall once more. My subject had been the old roads and tracks of Dorset, Ghost Roads as I call them. Many of them are old friends, going back to boyhood, and I love to trace and retrace them, on the map and on the ground, and to talk about them.

My hunting has had a recessional, evening quality about it this millennial season. I have stopped visiting, and we have sold the lorry. I just hunt to please myself, with the same pack, and some of the same families, that I started with more than half a century ago, picking the meets I like, and staying out not a second longer than I wish to. Age has its privileges.

Last Sunday, we met at Plush. Thomas Hardy called it Flintcomb Ash, no doubt meaning to convey the starve-acre nature of the farm work that poor Tess was condemned to when she lodged there.

Today, and in reality, it is a lovely place, a small village, remote, folded in downland, and nestling just below that prehistoric arterial route, the Great Ridgeway. If you lay a ruler on the map of the county and bisect its length and depth you will locate Plush. In more than one sense, it is in the very heart of Dorset.

Great open fields, once sheep-walks, now, sadly, mostly ploughed, mean that you can get everywhere, see everything. Stone-Age man has left his mark, he buried his dead there, and no doubt sketched out the network of paths and trackways that countless generations of travellers and local farmers have since made permanent.

Much of the morning we were threading a long bank and hedge that the Saxons established some 1,500 years ago, and which is still a parish boundary. More than once we followed the track of the medieval Dorchester to London road, now long deserted, but through centuries the familiar route of teams of packhorses. What used to be a peopled landscape has been abandoned by the modern world – there were just the hounds, always in view, and us.

It was a blissful half day, in which not much happened – there is a shortage of foxes round here this season; the sun had shone, and Dandy had behaved beautifully. I was paddling him and a led-horse in some nameless tributary of the River Piddle, getting the worst of the mud from off their legs, and giving them a chance to drink, while my kind neighbour was busy extracting his lorry from a soggy verge. It dawned on me that I am enjoying hunting these days as much as I ever have done.

MARCH

When Parson Evans, as our country history tells, built the wall round two sides of this property in the eighteenth century, he built on his own land, leaving a selvage on his northern boundary, which carries the church path. I would not care to go to war on whether or not that path now actually belongs to me, but I recognise a duty to keep it free of weeds and regularly swept.

This is one of the worst jobs in the calendar. It is such a long path and so dank. The good parson no doubt recognised that one can at the same time love one's privacy and one's neighbour – the 8ft wall protected him and his from the eyes of churchgoers. It performs the same grateful, tactful service now; but not a ray of sunlight ever strikes that path, and it is a sad, back-aching business shovelling up the moss that thrives there, pulling the weeds and sweeping up the fallen leaves.

I usually do the job in time for Easter, and again at Harvest Festival, but one recent Tuesday morning it seemed right to tackle the chore early. As if the place were not dismal enough in its own right, my friend Paul was to make his last visit to the church by that route in the afternoon. For the path is traditionally the way of the dead.

It had been a dreadful time, ten days earlier, one I can never forget. Home after a magic day's hunting, all cleaned up, counting in my mind the various obstacles Dandy had jumped to perfection, I was hugging myself and looking forward to telling my wife all about it. As I awaited her return from being a grandmother in London, the telephone rang. How can one tell when that damned bell is going to signal a switch of points in life?

Paul, who had also been hunting, with a neighbouring pack, riding, as we heard later, with especial recklessness, had suddenly taken himself off from among us without notice. There was everything to be done, and I, with several other neighbours and friends, had at least the advantage of feeling useful in the face of such a tragedy. There was much dire business to be crammed into the following week, and it started, appropriately enough, with a black eye.

Wanting to be shot of the horses for the day I was leading them out to grass. Bella – she with the broken knees now nearly mended – unintentionally, no doubt, threw her head at me, her jawbone catching me above the eye. Dandy, in my other hand, as if following a plan pre-concerted with his sister, improved the occasion by immediately placing one of his large feet confidingly on top of one of mine. I tripped, and fell, streaming blood, full-length flat, face-first into the mud. Both horses scarpered, and it began to rain.

Thus an unhappy week started, and that is how it came about that I was to be found, with a rainbow eye and a heavy heart, doing the worst job of the year on the morning of the Tuesday following.

There had been a happy interlude. We spent a short weekend in my very favourite city. Florence, I adore the place. The first time I ever left this country was to take myself off there as a rather over-serious young man, inspired by Benvenuto Cellini's account of how he cast his Perseus, and I have been there as often as possible since.

On this occasion, we went at the invitation of my younger stepdaughter and her Italian husband, to enjoy with them the privilege of a tour conducted by an expert of atelier and the like, looking at furniture and fittings for their Milan flat. Walking those streets, revisiting those storied places, where at every corner turned you draw your breath at the beauty, interest and antiquity of the scene, sleeping above the Arno, and waking to find Brunelleschi's incomparable dome swimming on the skyline, enjoying wine and food that I prefer to any other, was a pleasant change indeed. It made up for having one's eye blacked by a little minx of a horse who has not done a day's work since the eclipse, and brought us home with lighter hearts than could otherwise have been possible.

APRIL

The old adage that a boy should always carry sixpence, a penknife and a length of knot-free string in his pocket (have I got the list right?) has a modern counterpart I find – never drive anywhere without a bin-liner and a piece of binder-twine. The other day, hurrying into Sherborne for an early appointment with the dentist, I saw a dead fox lying in the road on the outskirts of the village of Longburton. So, instead of worrying about the dentist and his dire potholing, I was fretting about that sleeping beauty – so hoping it would survive north Dorset's muted rush hour and still be untouched on my return journey. Roadside casualties, sometimes so dignified and peaceful, deserve better than the squalor of being squashed.

I was in luck; she still lay there, pristine, beautiful, a slight snarl on her mask taking up almost half of the less busy side of the road. I realised with a shock that she was full to bursting with cubs and milk – she was enormous, stiff as a spade from the tag of her outstretched brush to her whiskers, and immensely heavy. How lucky I thought, that she and her brood had all died, so suddenly, together, like Macduff's family 'at one fell swoop'. Into the bin-liner she went, to join a knot of household waste-bags at some unsuspecting roadside gate in the next village, awaiting collection later in the morning. No doubt that was a municipally incorrect act, but I felt that I had done a good deed, not least by the residents of Longburton.

A recent rare but by no means rare enough, visit to London found me sitting on a sand-bin in Royal Avenue SW3, while my wife foraged on the further side of the King's Road. I had opted to risk threatening rain in preference to being deafened and stifled in GAP. Neither the shop, nor the Royal Borough evidently, wished to accommodate visitors with anywhere to sit as one dreams of the last train west, and has nightmares about missing it – hence the sand bin. It made quite a comfortable seat, if rather like a misericord: the rake of the sloping lid would certainly ensure that you slipped quietly to the ground if you should in fact actually fall asleep.

I enjoyed the company of the pigeons, although ordered by a fussy notice not to feed them. The bronzed necks of some of them reminded me of the purpose of our visit: a reception in the Natural History Museum that evening to honour my grandmother's grandfather, John Gould, the great Victorian naturalist. Among other wonders in a remarkable life, he had invented a way of reproducing the metallic colouring of his beloved humming birds on paper. He would have been amused, as I was, to have watched the perennially optimistic courting of the cock-birds and the incurable 'headaches' of the hens. Such cavorting wing-dragging and cooing – the whole thing forgotten in an instant at the crumple of a paper bag, and the suggestion of an illicit crumb.

My wife emerged from GAP an hour later, pleased with some skimpy bargain. We walked the length of Sloane Street to The Scotch House, where I collected a pair of trousers in the Eliott tartan, which I may wear, I hope, in my mother's name, to enliven Dorset dinner parties – and my wife bought a pair of Church's excellent shoes. Then it was back again, on foot, the length of Sloane Street to the King's Road, doubts having set in about the size of the said skimpy garment. Finally, we gave ourselves the great treat of tea on the top floor of Peter Jones, with its wonderful roofscape view, and windows that you can actually open.

The museum was everything we had hoped for, and we caught our train. I loathe the noise, dirt, airlessness and perpetual bustle of London, but have to admit it, we had a lovely day.

I do not hold St Patrick in especial reverence, in my opinion he left too many 'snakes' at large in Ireland. But I celebrated his day this year by riding Bella for the first time since she broke her knees last August. She stepped generously away from the mounting block and trotted down the drive, ears cocked, as bright as butter, seeming to want nothing so much in the whole world as to go wherever it might be that we were going. It is a rare and loveable characteristic in a horse – as in a wife.

JUNE

What fleeting lives our boon companions have. Was it really nine years ago that Perdita arrived? It seems no time at all since I first set eyes on her. A stray who just pitched up in the village, then she was a puppy, game for anything: now she is a little old lady, somewhat grizzled about the chops. She takes life easily, regrets it if she gets caught up in rough play, and is like a snail on the rare occasion that she still comes riding with me.

Some people who hear us call her 'Perdie' think of the great gunsmith, and suppose I shoot, but the truth is both of us are gun-shy. I detest loud noises, the whole business of Army gunnery was torture. But Perdie is far worse, the slightest 'pop', a single shot two fields away, has her diving for cover, tail glued between her legs, beyond comfort for an hour or more.

As I write, thunder begins to stumble round the Dorset Heights: Perdie, deserting her bone on the lawn, climbs two flights of stairs to lie on the floor behind me, panting and anxious. We made a terrible mistake on the eve of the millennium, going out and forgetting about the fireworks. She was beside herself when we returned in the early hours of the present century, and had half gnawed through the kitchen door. She may have forgotten it, but we do not forgive ourselves.

Like many lurchers, Perdita is a strange mixture of timid toad and fearless hunter. We used to laugh at her puppyish attempts to catch roe-deer. This was an error, we could have trained her off deer, as my wife did in a few minutes when she took too close an interest in our sheep. All too soon she learnt to pull deer down, and, if you could not get to her, would hang on to a hamstring until the wretched creature, twice her weight and more, gave up the fight and died.

I forget how many tussles we had with deer. One Sunday morning when I was riding and leading, I thought on a safe route, a doe crossed the road just ahead of us, and Perdie was off. By the time I had found someone to mind the horses she had the deer down in a stream in a steep-sided gully. Diving through a meuse under a hedge, I scrambled down and separated them. On another occasion, when I caught up with her, she was sparring with a mature buck. It was an extraordinary sight, she intent on getting to the creature's hind quarters, trying it seemed to get between his legs and trip him.

He, equally determined to fend her off, was well armed to do so. Perdie still has a scar on her flank as a memento of that particular engagement.

Thinking of Perdie ageing drove me back to *The Jungle Book*, which I have not looked at in 60 years. I remember being desolated as a child when Akela, 'turned from grey to milky white with age', was displaced as leader of his pack. It was a useful lesson in the realities of the natural world.

As Perdie grows old, other animals take unprecedented liberties. Cats, who would previously not have dreamt of setting a paw or twitching a whisker on her manor, sit and blatantly wash themselves wherever it may suit them about the garden. A cock pheasant struts his stuff on the lawn, and crows all round the house. Deer actually come up the drive, and graze in the paddocks as if they belonged there. Any day I expect rabbits to recolonise my vegetable patch (what fun Perdie and I used to have playing at 'Mr McGregor' when she was a puppy, before she banished them).

The 'radar screen', which only she can see, beside her beanbag in the kitchen, still functions well. She knows just what goes on outside the house, can smell her Friday butcher's bone approaching at 100yds, and is out of her trap-door and down the drive to meet a faithful friend from the village in a flash. But, as the jungle closes in, this once great huntress keeps her bed. At least our young horses, the oldest foaled in the same year that Perdie came to us, will 'Grow old along with me'.

AUGUST

Bucket-and-spade holidays are among the earliest of childhood memories. We children, I was then the youngest of three, and very much bobbing in my siblings' wake, would be packed into the back seat of my mother's Morris Eight, with the nursemaid in front, and off we would go for a week at, perhaps, Swanage. We lived at South Petherton in Somerset then, and no doubt my parents rang the changes, with so much of the coastline in reach, but all my seaside memories are of Swanage, and, for me, the place has a halo on it that nothing can remove.

I remember the sand and sea of course, but wonderful things happened on the beach. On one never-to-be-forgotten day the lifeboat was run out, on another a shark was landed. A kilted piper sometimes skirled up and down the strand. There must have been a sovereign's birthday on one of our holidays, as a field-gun was wheeled out and fired, and often a sculptor made amazing statues in wet sand behind a screen – you paid a penny I think to be allowed to look at them.

Later in life I soon enough tired of the beach and its attractions: I have never seen the point of swimming. But if I shut my eyes now I can still hear the delighted cries of children against the sound of gently breaking waves... at Swanage.

We are just returned from a week in Santa Margherita Ligure, on the Gulf of Genoa, where buckets and spades were not in requisition. True, there are beaches there, where, for as little as £50 a day, you may purchase the sort of space and privacy that would satisfy a nesting gannet, but those of us who wanted to swim were able to do so from a yacht. That same *Quicksilver* which my wife and I had helped collect from her builders on Lake Erie and deliver to New York last year was moored in the harbour.

Our apartment, generously lent, was in a villa the colour of baked custard, with dark green shutters. It had a squash-court-sized balcony, where, when there was nothing else to do, one might lie in the shade and read, and listen to the sea and to the sounds of Italy. The Italians have done their best to destroy their lovely country with noise – and failed. It doesn't do to let the clamour get to you, you have to school yourself to revel in its ghastliness, and learn to laugh at it. I, who crave quiet above almost anything, adore Italy: it is a paradox explained by the beauty of the place and the charm of its people.

One morning as I lay there, a voluble lady with a mobile telephone burst onto the balcony of the villa above us on the steep hill face. She might have been singing, in grand opera. The volume and extravagant modulations of her voice, the wide gestures with her free hand, the length of the performance, the wild laughter, the extraordinary artless outpouring, she was like a bird in full song. I did not understand a word of what she said, but it gave me immense pleasure. What would have constituted, emotionally, a day's work and a week's wonder for a phlegmatic Englishman, was evidently no more than the small change of an idle morning for this signora on her holidays, passing the time of day with her gossip at home.

On one memorable day, with the boat's crew, we walked the fairly rugged track over the shoulder of Monte Portofino to the landlocked site of an eighth-century monastery by the cliff's foot at San Fruttuoso. The weather was doubtful, but we had decided to risk it. Half way to our destination, and our lunch, colossal thunder overtook us – we were soaked. We were drenched again on the return trip. Milan, we later learnt, was actually flooded that afternoon, with a downpour not seen in years. What would have been a demanding walk in fair weather had turned into quite an adventure.

On our final morning, whilst the others swam from the rocks, I walked down to Santa Margherita, to enjoy a *pinguino*, and to say goodbye to the boat and to her crew. A *pinguino* is an ice-cream that, before your eyes, is dipped into hot chocolate, and is indescribably delicious. I had a last look at the incomparable Bay of Tigulio, with mountains lining the shore like a rank of sized soldiers, shading away to the south. If Italy assaults the ear it certainly requites the eye; or at least the Ligurian coast does. Nothing on that teeming shore seemed out of place, vulgar, or ugly. I am patriotic by nature, and draw no comparisons, but I found myself, as ever, envying Italian style, taste, craftsmanship and grace.

OCTOBER

Something happened in this small North Dorset village early last month, which beggars the imagination, or ought to. 'I think that it is awful cheek to believe that they can behave like that: we never had anything of that sort here before' was a typical reaction, that of my 92-year-old mother. Our Post Office, which had served the village for well over 100 years one supposes, and had been run by our postmistress for the last 35, was suddenly closed down.

The first that I heard about it was at midday one Friday. There was a message: would I ring the chairman of our parish meeting? He told me what I could scarcely believe, that our faithful postmistress had been visited by her manager from Taunton on the previous day. She had found the recently installed computer terminal impossible to cope with, the worry of it was undermining her health: he had a letter of resignation in his hand: she signed it.

And so this brave lady, who had endured no fewer than seven robberies in recent years, two of them with violence, stood her ground, and kept the service to the village and for her employers going, was persuaded at the point of a pen to sign away both her livelihood and her beloved occupation. Our Post Office was to close on Monday, the village was to have no warning, and our postmistress no period of notice to serve out. She their employee, and we their customers, were discarded without ceremony, on the moment. "Off with his head!' said the Red Queen' – we might just as well all have been with Alice in a nightmare Wonderland.

What could we do? What can anyone do when officialdom pounces, out of a blue September sky, so skilfully declaring war just as the world shuts down for the weekend? Some of us tried to persuade our postmistress to withdraw the resignation so promptly and suddenly secured from her by her employer – she being at the time alone, unadvised and unsupported. But she had had enough. Not for anything would she risk being obliged to use that wretched computer for one day more.

We, of course, tried to contact Post Office Counters Ltd. The telephone directory gave a Bristol address for 'customer enquiries', but this was a blind. The number given alongside proved to be in Yorkshire, and produced the usual nauseating mantra, too familiar in both senses of that word, along the lines of 'Hello, Kirstie speaking, how may I assist you?'

Needless to say 'Kirstie' could not assist us; her computer knew nothing of our problem, and she was not allowed to identify a contact nearer home. Pressed, she promised to get the local manager to ring; she rang back later naming him, and saying that he would call – he didn't. Time ran out, we were into the weekend, and the village – that part of it at least that had heard the news – was in shock.

Monday dawned, and those who had not felt the tremors on the grapevine or been to church or chapel, had the benefit of learning the news from the following notice on the blind, locked shop door. 'Please note this Post Office is now closed. Post Office Counters Ltd. apologises for any inconvenience caused to its customers. The nearest Post Office is at ...', naming a village over three miles away.

On Tuesday, for the first time in 30 years, when my mother took her customary walk to pass the time of day with her old friend and neighbour at the village shop, she was not able to draw her pension, and supply herself with cash.

NOVEMBER

The heights of various well-remembered horses are marked on our stable wall. Topping them all at not far off 18hh was Oliver, a massive grey that my father hunted in the 1950s, and that people round here still speak of. He used to go to be clipped at Minterne by the late Lady Digby's groom, whose tiny daughter, now a grandmother, hanging gamely onto the handle of the twitch, he would dangle in the air while his head was being done. George Fripp and I have been reminiscing about those days.

George was born at Minterne, where his father was a carter on the home farm. He went to the village school until he was 11, and then to the school in Cerne Abbas until 14, walking daily on the in those days rough, now smooth, busy road – more than two miles each way. From the age of 12 he started to work at weekends in the stables at Minterne, before working there full-time when his schooling finished.

Graduating from stable boy to clipping and plaiting, and then to second-horseman, he more than once in the 1930s took Lord Digby's horses to Mentmore, for a few days with the Whaddon Chase, travelling by train from Evershot. On a Boxing Day, more than 300 horses would turn out for the meet in Wing market-place, and George would be one of upwards of 70 second-horsemen. Once, at the end of the day, when he had two horses to get home some ten miles to Mentmore, in the dark, from he knew not where, Lord Rosebery said, 'You ride my horse, and lead Lord Digby's: it will take you to its stable.' It did.

George married just before the Second World War. He met Sally at a dance, here in our Village Hall. They would bicycle the eight miles or so from her home in Sydling St Nicholas, and, when the dance ended, at maybe 2a.m., bicycle back again, George getting to Minterne perhaps just in time to change, and turn his horses out for cubhunting. Sally and he were to have four daughters, and ten grandchildren, all but one of them boys. They have 13 great-grandchildren at the last count, and celebrated their 61st wedding anniversary earlier this year.

War brought changes. The great house at Minterne became a naval hospital, and George transferred to working with the cart-horses and, among other things, helping with Lord Digby's famous Guernsey herd. He went to enlist, but was turned down, being needed on the land, and served in the Home Guard.

I remember once, shortly after the war, hacking up with my father to a meet of the Cattistock at Dogbury Gate. Lady Digby, a familiar figure, riding side-saddle of course, was out with her grandson, the young Winston Churchill, in tow. She would have had a kind word for us children, no doubt recognising my pony, bought on her recommendation. (It was not just an excellent first pony that my sister and I had to thank her for: its previous owner, whom we might not otherwise have met, has been my brother-in-law these 45 years.) Lord Digby no longer hunted in those postwar days, but I met him once, on my way to the forge in Cerne, he with an electric float, delivering his Guernsey milk in the village. It was only when I got home that I learnt that the kindly, if well-spoken, milkman, with whom I had been passing the time of day, and who seemed to know my pony, was the future Knight of the Garter.

George was running the hunting stable at Minterne by then. When Lady Digby's hunting days ended, Sally Fripp kept house for her at the Abbey in Cerne, and George saw to the garden and drove her car. They were with her through the 14 years of her widowhood, until she died in 1978. Many are the stories that they have to tell of 'Lady', of her unforgettable character, and kindness, and of their devotion to her.

The Fripps live in Back Lane, Cerne Abbas, now. Their house stands a bit above the village, a window exactly framing the blue clock face on the church tower. Behind the church and the Abbey stands the mass of Giant's Head Hill, where George used to summer 'Lady's' hunters, and where he taught the young Winston to jump gorse bushes on his pony; beyond lies the neighbouring parish of Minterne Magna, in which he was born, 90 years ago last week.

JANUARY

'Chequebook!!' roared the huntsman in his most commanding tone. A small dark-coloured hound, on the point of sidling off to join a couple that could be heard hunting on their own account in the bottom of the 'goyle', returned hurriedly to the pack. We were looking out across Bin Combe, at the foot of Dunkery Hill, and, as so often on Exmoor, the business-end of the hunt was laid out below us like a tapestry. Hunting on the moor is such a treat, if you enjoy that sort of thing.

I had been watching Chequebook through the day. It is a trick that I taught myself early on as a hunting correspondent – a cheap trick you might think – to identify a hound at the meet, and follow its fortunes. If we should have a blank day, or the hunting not amount to much, then at least I would have something to write about. I have also found that it helps concentration, and adds to the interest and enjoyment.

This particular little bitch gave me a lot of fun. She was easy enough to pick out, being an inch at least shorter at the shoulder, and, although chubbier, lighter in build than the rest of the pack (all bitches): except for the tip of her stern, and a triangle below it, she was as black as your hat. Recently drafted from a local pack of foxhounds, she could hardly believe her luck, one supposed, in actually being encouraged in what she felt herself to have been born to do. For I was visiting the Quantock Staghounds, and they were visiting in their neighbour's country.

Chequebook had a good day. She had a struggle to keep up with her fitter colleagues, but was generally somewhere near the middle of the pack – and, when it split, she was to be found in the virtuous half, at the huntsman's heels. The other heroine of the occasion was Lucy, 'Sure-footed Lucy' I call her, an old and valued friend, lent me by another such, once or twice a season for a treat.

It was the usual story of riding on the moor, but with the going underfoot this wet season worse than ever. Down improbable places and up impossible ones, vice-versa, ditto, ditto, and so on all day. 'Ride a local horse, follow a likely looking pilot, grab the neck-strap, and shut your eyes' has been my rule for surviving in such countries, and it has served me well.

'Typical chestnut mare' I said incautiously across the table to my *vis-à-vis* at a recent luncheon party, speaking of Bella, our youngest and trickiest horse. The auburn lady on my right bridled – 'There is a lot of nonsense talked about them' she said, meaning, I believe, to say 'us'. 'Handle her properly, and you won't breed anything better than a chestnut filly.' And I really think that she may be right: but I cannot forget that my wife burst into tears on the morning seven years ago when I told her that Daisy had a chestnut foal with her in her box, and that it was female. The general view seems to be that a chestnut mare means trouble: I say nothing about auburn ladies.

Bella is an adorable horse in the stables (unless it should happen that you want to clip her, when she is downright dangerous), and the brightest horse to ride I have ever sat on. She had brought me to something that I never thought to do – keeping a hack, solely for the pleasure of riding about the place on it, but I doubt she will ever make an honest hunter like her brother – you just do not know what she will do next. Show her anything that she is not used to and she has a fit of the vapours: she once actually sat down when confronted by a jump that boggled her. God knows what she would make of Exmoor.

This is the first season in ten years when I find myself not regularly employed as a hunting correspondent – I miss it more even than I expected. It was not a profession I planned to embark on, and I turned the offer of it down at first. But, as Surtees said, writing is like taking snuff, it is difficult to leave off. Once I had filed my first hunt report, seen it in print, with some outstanding pictures, I just could not have enough of it.

Ten or a dozen times a season I would set off, usually on a Friday evening or Saturday morning, for some distant rendezvous with an unknown horse, to ride among strangers in a country that was new to me. I was never given less than a first-class horse to ride, never had less than the kindest of welcomes. Riding into covert with the huntsman, as I was sometimes allowed to do, was dreamlike.

With a bit of effort I can recall every single horse that I rode, and think with gratitude of the moment of arriving in the saddle when you feel straight away that you are on a strong, fit, confident, competent and optimistic animal. And I can call to mind quite a few individual hounds: the most fresh in memory being Chequebook, who I like to think of as 'living happily ever after' in her new home at Bagborough.

MARCH

Mrs Jellyby is alive and well, and flourishing in Blair's Britain. She, you will remember, was the character in *Bleak House* who was so high-mindedly obsessed with the problems of the natives of far off Borrioboola-Gha that she completely neglected her own children. Thus today we are subjected to endless 'green' pieties, not least from the young, about the Amazon rainforest, pandas and the polar ice-cap, yet our beautiful country lanes are strewn with hideous litter – crisp packets, plastic bottles, and much worse.

What would parents be at, that they give schoolchildren trash food, and take no interest in what happens to the wrappings; and why are schools so negligent or feeble that they do not teach their charges to behave better? Are we really rearing a generation that has no social conscience, no aesthetic eye? These are the thoughts that trouble me as I climb off 16.2hh for the umpteenth time to pick up some unsightly piece of garbage in a favourite place, to pocket it and take it home.

Of course by no means all the litter-bugs are children. A bicycle wheel, left in a broad inviting verge, was not just a lethal hazard but a puzzle: how did that bicyclist get home? One does not have to be Einstein to imagine how a horse's hoof might have driven through those spokes and been caught in it, and to picture the mayhem that might have followed for both horse and rider, and for any passing traffic.

'Some-when' last autumn, as they say round here, or 'back along', a land-press, otherwise known as a furrow-breast, jumped out of the bucket of a tractor, as it was driven in too cavalier a fashion down the hill that leads into this village. A land-press is a small ring-roller that may be fitted onto the side of a plough so as to smooth the furrows made on its previous circuit. Landing on the tarmac, this one shattered into 50 or so jagged cast-iron fragments, which the tractor driver thought it right just to heave onto the verge, and apparently, to forget.

I did not witness the incident, but nothing of that sort goes un-remarked in any country area, and it was not difficult to learn, from a jerked thumb, to whom the pile of lethal scrap belonged. But this was no time to be bothering farmers, on the rack with foot and mouth. I was determined somehow to shift the lethal wreckage, which looked like the collapsed ribcage of some gigantic animal, waiting for the grass to grow through it and perfect the trap; it is a verge I often ride on to save shoe-iron.

I removed them a week ago, and hard morning's work it was.

There is a narrow road of great charm that meanders west from this village, connecting us with the neighbouring parish, we call it Kennels Lane. No one knows when and where the kennels stood, but the name passes down the generations by word of mouth, and will do so no doubt as long as there are people who take an interest in such things.

It is a particularly favourite ride of mine, as it leads towards the Ridgeway. A tributary of the Caundle Brook runs, deeply embanked, first on one side of the road and then upon the other. In season it is full of flowers and bird-song, and other wildlife. One quiet Sunday morning, a summer or so ago, as I have recounted on this page, a roe-deer was silly enough to cross the road under our noses. I released it from Perdita's jaws in the bottom of that stream bed.

Perdie is no longer able to keep up with horses, but she comes with me when I return on foot to pick up heavy litter spotted, abandoned, in that lovely place. On these occasions our usual roles become reversed. It is she then that strains at the leash impatiently, I that endlessly investigate around and under bushes. She seems to say, 'Come on for goodness sake, surely you have done with that, we haven't got all day!'

Six months ago, a heavy-looking plastic bag, noticed when riding by in the morning, turned out to contain the four lower legs of an ox, severed at the knee. Last week, another bag looking unpleasantly familiar, but this time tossed across the stream and very difficult to get to, contained the heads and feet of two roe-deer. It was a nightmare moment looking into it, like opening the door to Bluebeard's den.

A blissful day was spent watching undergraduates playing arena polo, in that interval of halcyon weather we all enjoyed in February. Not least of the pleasures of the day had been the company – they might have been our own children, ten years back, so sunny tempered, so enthusiastic, so well mannered, so much enjoying and ornamenting the occasion. As we all trooped off, in twilight, for the prize-giving in an indoor school I looked back at the vacated grandstand: it, and the ground round it, was a snowfield of discarded paper cups and napkins.

Have I answered one of my own questions? It is perhaps our fate as adults to pick up litter for the young, until they have grown aware of what is due to the world immediately around them, and discovered that being thought 'cool' is not after all the only thing that matters in this life.

MAY

We have been enjoying the company of a Lucas terrier called Freddie, who came to stay here for a week. He is, aesthetically, the perfect complement to Perdita, if not always her boon companion – it is a classic combination, a longdog and a terrier, celebrated by Cecil Aldin in his delightful short book *Sleeping Partners*, by Landseer in *Dignity and Impudence*, and which romps through the pages of Somerville and Ross.

No doubt they would make a useful sporting combination too, if Perdie were only younger, but she finds Freddie too boisterous by half, and has, these days, only a fraction of his inexhaustible appetite for play. When she has had enough and wants to keep to her beanbag, she just lifts one corner of her lip, showing a small triangle of ivory, and Freddie gets the hint.

I myself have failed totally to devise any way of putting Freddie down. From the moment first thing in the morning, when he laps busily round my slippered feet like the on-run of an incoming tide, until he goes off sentry-duty last thing at night, I am aware of his presence. By day he is a shackle to my ankle, in the evening a muffler to my feet. With Freddie as a houseguest, peace is a dream. It is a miracle I am writing this.

Freddie seems to have a penchant for doing, and especially undoing, the outdoor things I do. When I plant out old house-bulbs in the shrubbery I find that he has loyally exhumed them, every one. He stands there, proudly, wagging his stumpy little tail, barking excitedly, expecting, not to be cursed, but to be praised for winning first prize in a treasure hunt.

When I carefully lift specially manicured turf in the meadow, to abolish yet another flower-bed, the moment my back is turned the perfect square that I have cut is converted into a bomb crater. Who told this little town dog that a man with digging tools must be on a rat hunt, and needing help? What powerful instincts these terriers have; the French did not call them 'earth dogs' for nothing.

On his last morning with us I suggested that he come to unlock the church with me, and he inspired Perdie to join us – usually she thinks this chore far too tame, and quite beneath her notice; not worth getting out of bed for, as they say. Instead of taking the short route through the orchard we followed the path that winds under our northern boundary wall

It is a dank, dreary place, the way of the dead, with never a touch of warmth or light. Returning, Perdie was at my heel, but Freddie was AWOL, 'digging up bones in the churchyard no doubt' was my uncharitable thought. But a whistle brought him belting round the corner, a little rough-haired ray of sunshine. I suddenly realised that I would miss him – miss finding him an unexpected cushion in my chair, a little puddle of puzzled patience at my feet if I should be so uncool as to sit down for a moment to enjoy a book, or a pert centrepiece on my table, his footprints illustrating every single page of my work. Who can resist being hero-worshipped?

Country air seemed to agree with Freddie. One morning his temporary mistress said 'He eats like a house' – I asked her to repeat the phrase just to make sure I had not misheard it. I do think that the world has a lot to thank Mrs Malaprop for – to borrow a phrase from Dr Johnson, she adds to the gaiety of nations. A lady who some years ago used to visit here referred to the little devils who beaver away in the ancient timbers of this house, and which you can actually hear at work at this time of year, as 'Black Watch Beetles'. I love to picture the little fellows in their bonnets, kilts and sporrans, with dirks stuck in their stockings. It makes me feel quite positive about them, as they chisel on, and the dust from their dire tunnelling falls all around me.

JUNE

The notebooks that my mother kept during the half-century that she lived in this house record the comings and goings, and doings generally, of the birds in our garden. She loved the outdoors, followed the changing seasons, noted the weather and what the 'glass' was doing.

I read in them of shocking events, such as Perdie 'stealing seven eggs that the fishmonger had left, taking them one by one to consume on the lawn'; of tragedies such as a flycatcher hanging herself on a horsehair caught on a rose-thorn, the widower, even weeks later, returning regularly to the nest, empty except for three cold eggs; of a starling called Telecom because he so accurately mimicked a ringing bell, and a young tail-less magpie called Toby, one of the many regular beggars at her back door. Second only to children, and the company of family and neighbours, her passion was animals and birds.

By Christmas, she was too ill to enjoy the song thrush that, right through January, every morning, gave my wife and me a full-throated concert with the rising sun from just across the lawn outside our bedroom window. It perched dangerously, on a leafless tree, and I have no doubt that it was a sparrow-hawk that suddenly silenced it – the same that haunts this place the year round, like some legendary ogre demanding its tribute of youth and beauty. I met it a few days later in our kitchen yard, causing a scandal among a crowd of blackbirds and sparrows.

That was a bad week at the back end of February, when we lost our songster, for, on one desolate evening, having waited fruitlessly for three hours for an ambulance, I took my mother by car to a nursing home. We had so hoped that she would see out her days here, but, almost exactly 50 years after she first arrived, a wife and mother in the prime of life, I took her from the home she loved, and placed her in the care of strangers. It was a hateful duty, and a hateful day.

When my mother died, it chanced I was on my own. Returning to an empty house, in the evening, before inevitably picking up the telephone and re-engaging with the outside world, I could think of nothing better than to go and keep company with the horses, who are so companionable, contended and reassuring, when they are at grass. While with them I heard the first cuckoo of the year, it was 6 May, a date noted by my mother in 1979 as being 'very late'.

Born, like Nelson, in the parsonage at Burnham Thorpe, my mother was the youngest but one of nine children. 'I do not advocate large families' she used to say – hers cannot have been a particularly easy childhood, at the tail end of such a brood. Another familiar saying was 'I had quite enough of Drake and Nelson as a child' – her father's uncle was the last Sir Francis Drake. But 'England, home and duty', to adapt a phrase from the Nelsonian song, was very much the theme of her upbringing, and her life.

She and her five sisters, all to be women of marked character, went together to Roedean, the boys to Brighton College: school fees cannot have been the problem they are now, my grandparents were not moneyed people. The eldest boy went into the Norfolk Regiment, and served in two world wars, the other two sought their fortunes as farmers in South Africa. All those nine children married. I have more first cousins, here and in Africa, than I can easily number or put names to.

My mother was the last survivor in her generation of that large Norfolk family, the only one to see this century. Her funeral seemed to be the final closing of a book, one which I am grateful to have read, a story of Empire, a vanished world, and vanished values. Midsummer's Day would have been her 93rd birthday.

There were more people than there is regular seating for in our little church at her memorial service. Family came from far and wide of course, but, like my father, my mother was much thought of hereabouts. Through more than 30 years of widowhood she never quite gave up as the doctor's wife; almost to the end, she would walk down the drive, scorning a stick, to be the first to call on new arrivals. She was never the last to know, or slowest offering help, should illness or misfortune overtake a neighbour.

We had more than 100 in the house for tea that afternoon – I wondered if the old place had seen such a crowd before, or such a crush. As I had run down from the church into our orchard, a flood of bluebells under a cloud of blossom, in a hurry to get the door unlocked and the teapots pouring, there was a thrush singing its heart out somewhere about the garden.

AUGUST

Bella, our homebred chestnut mare, now, unbelievably, nine years old and well over 16hh although I still think of her as a baby, gives us a lot of heartache: she keeps falling down. Not, of course, whilst I am on her back – even I, who find it very difficult to acknowledge any fault in her, would be tempted to give up on her if she did that – she falls down, as far as we can tell, when she falls asleep.

This does not matter in the winter, when she is in the stable on a deep bed, indeed we do not really know if she does it then. But on this hard ground, every morning it is a worry to know if we shall find her once again with a bloody off-side knee or near-hind pastern – always the same identical, diagonal stigmata – as has happened more than once this summer.

It is two years now since, on the morning of the eclipse, shying at a playful dog, she came down in the road, doing horrible injury to both her knees. Nursing her through her convalescence, under the skilled supervision of my wife, must account for the special bond that I have with that mare. So tricky in many ways, she endeared herself to me by the docility and trust with which she let me inject her, and clean and dress her wounds twice daily for goodness knows how long. Her brother Dandy, so much more tractable in every other way, would not have let me near him: he is a total coward with needles and the vet.

Some of our knowledgeable friends aver that the 'locking mechanism' in Bella's knees must have been damaged in the original fall – others say that there is no such mechanism. What is one to believe? Furthermore there is a complication. When the wounds were first being treated she reared up and cut her head open on a light-fitting, inflicting another deep wound on herself, which required stitches, festered, and took an age to heal. Did she in some way injure the part of her brain that governs balance?

If I were just reading this account, not writing it, I would no doubt say that it is foolish to persevere with such a horse. But, if she is still iffy as a hunter, she is the brightest hack I have ever sat on: I spend a lot of time, summer and winter, on her back, and she is very dear to me. It is out of the question to keep her in the stable round the year, or, I suppose, to keep her knees permanently protected, but is there nothing else that we could do to prevent her injuring herself, and why does she do it?

That London life has its compensations and its beauties I must grudgingly admit, since they sometimes come to mind. Years ago, when I was serving a sentence as a staff officer in the Ministry of Defence I was lucky enough to share an office that overlooked the river. Whilst I ought to have been busy planning the Third World War, I sometimes used to watch a pair of kestrels which had their nest high up on County Hall across the water. And in my lunch-hours I would trudge round Samuel Pepys's and Dr Johnson's haunts. Covent Garden was a particular favourite, especially the portico of the great barn of a church, St Paul's, built by Inigo Jones in the year that the diarist was born. I do not know a more storied or more evocative spot.

The potted Boswell, given to me by my father when I was 17 years old I see, has a picture of Covent Garden in the great doctor's day, as imagined by E.H. Shepard. His Pepys and Johnson were my Pepys and Johnson, his London my London, such is the power of a good illustrator on a young imagination.

But what has London, even Shepard's idealised London, got to compare with Dorset? This Monday morning, I was up early to meet the usual deadline, and beat the worst of the flies and of the sun. Prior to checking Bella's knees and getting her and her brother in for a ride in the cool of the day, I went to see how far up their poles my runner beans had climbed. And there, hanging between the bamboo tops, catching the still low sun, was a complete set of twelve perfect, large, *diamanté* cobwebs, lightly jewelled with dew. You can keep London.

SEPTEMBER

In Italy, small children get the same sort of attention as we reserve for dogs in this country. A baby is better than a paddock badge: you can go anywhere with a *bambino*. Wheeling my step-granddaughter in her pushchair on the quay at Santa Margherita Ligure, passers-by would greet us as though we were old friends. While total strangers admired Sophia, I could study the dogs that thrive in all improbable varieties in that seaside place.

I saw everything from a pair of huskies, eagerly dragging along a brown nymph in a bikini, to the tiniest dolly-mop of a lapdog, its head protruding from a swaying shopping bag, barking crossly at its owner's every pace. There were poodles galore, out-of-work terriers of all shapes and sizes, and even something halfway to being a lurcher. The owner of a beautiful yellow Labrador, consort of a dress-shop owner – we seemed somehow to spend a lot of time in dress shops – told me that, no, he didn't take the dog shooting, it was too sleepy. Dogs, I think, must be rather frustrated in Italy, but, like children, they are much cherished.

We had come to Santa off the yacht *Quicksilver*, she that my wife and I inexpertly helped crew on her maiden voyage from Lake Erie to New York two years ago; this time we joined her in Corsica, sailing to and off Sardinia.

One memorable night we spent close by Nelson's Grand Fleet anchorage in the shelter of the Maddalena Islands, named Agincourt after the vessel whose captain first surveyed it. It was on 19 January 1805 that Nelson heard from his frigates that the enemy was at sea. He left his favourite anchorage for the last time three hours later, for the 4,000 mile chase that was to end at Trafalgar. 'Darkness was falling. The *Victory* led through the narrow passage between the Biocian and Sardinian rocks' (Carola Oman's *Nelson*).

Our own departure from Agincourt Sound was less propitious. Strictly in the practical, not metaphorical, sense I am anchorman when on board *Quicksilver*. It is a job the skipper gives me, I assume, to keep me out of the cockpit at critical times, and to give me some sense of being useful.

There is nothing to it, you just tread a button in the deck to drop or raise the anchor, watching the chain, and signalling to the helmsman to alter speed or course if our bow is about to foul it.

As we weighed anchor, my eyes glued to the chain, I was oblivious of a drama unfolding aft. *Quicksilver*, disobedient to the helm, seemed to be rushing towards a recently arrived neighbouring yacht as though they were long-parted lovers. By the time I saw that our anchor was hooked round their chain it was too late to forestall a kiss. No serious harm was done, just a bent rail, but it was an example of how quickly sailing can turn to slapstick.

That evening, following the course taken by the grand fleet, we sailed in light winds under main and foresail off the Costa Smeralda, and I sat in a favourite place, astride the anchor fairlead (the sticky-out bit at the front). If I owned a yacht I would strap a saddle there, for, in any sort of sea, sitting there, you can dream of riding a courageous horse into battle over an endless line of drop fences. The sun was brilliant, but past its fiercest heat and dropping towards Sardinia's spectacular purple mountain frieze, the spray on my face, added to the illusion of high adventure. I am no sailor, but with fair weather, few responsibilities, and the right pills (I have been sick in harbour before now) for sheer exhilaration in the open air, sailing takes some beating.

Another treat awaited us at home, Dorset Opera were staging Verdi's *Macbeth*. In case you have jumped to the wrong conclusion and think that Dorset Opera must be hedge opera, let me tell you that it is an aesthetic miracle performed annually at Sherborne School by a wide circle of experts and enthusiasts, a production of extraordinary quality, with professional soloists. Every year we go it seems better than the last: this year was no exception.

You will have twigged that although I affect to smile at the Italians' love of babies, it is something that, in truth, I envy and admire. There can be few more telling renderings of it than Macduff's heartbroken lament for his murdered children at the start of the final act of *Macbeth*. In the original 'What, all my pretty chickens and their dam, at one fell swoop?' (how Elizabethan theatre-goers must have been struck by that phrase now part of the small change of our language); or as the librettist has it: '*Ah, la paterna mano*'. For me this is the finest thing in the whole opera – Verdi's interpretation of his compatriots' most admirable and attractive foible.

OCTOBER

It is like that cut out cardboard dressing-up game we had as children, where you could give a grenadier a tutu, or a duchess football boots, the reflection of my own upper half in the glass before me is completed by a sensible tweed skirt, brogues, and lisle stockings. I am at the hairdresser's, where the clients sit opposite each other, separated by a line of dressing tables. Every now and then, as ladies get moved from one instrument of torture to another, a different pair of legs completes my seated portrait. The game is still fun, and I enjoy the hairdresser's, they take *Country Life*, it is the one spot on earth where I can look forward to be being, ever so slightly, lionised. Roy's is on the first floor at the abbey end of Cheap Street. Whilst 'Mrs Roy' gave me a trim and we exchange news I take in the roofscape across the way. Roofscapes in old towns so often have unconscious harmony, different ages, styles and materials blend together, details please the eye. It is well-mannered neighbourly English architecture: Sherborne is a well-mannered town; we who know it appreciate the fact.

Just in view is the sign that swings outside my tailors, the Joseph Weld Hospice Charity Shop. Colonel Sir Joseph Weld was a great figure in Dorset through much of my life. At Sandhurst with his son, the present *chatelain* of Lulworth, I was lucky enough to be roped in occasionally to partner one of his daughters.

I remember particularly a dance in Dorchester barracks when he set about seriously quizzing me, a callow subaltern whose views were not worth tuppence, whilst doing his kindly best to get me drunk. He had an extraordinary knack of making one feel at the same time both very small and incredibly important. A week or so later I appeared before him, defending one of my soldiers, at Wareham Magistrates Court. I cannot believe that anyone who had stood the full battery of his charm or met the gimlet twinkle of his eye could ever forget Joe Weld.

For years I and many of my friends had our hair cut by Mr Palmer further up Cheap Street. He was a dear man, I miss his talk, and the old-fashioned ambience of his family-run shop. Having served his barber's apprenticeship in that same street he found himself swept up and across the world by war, to scenes and adventures that as a boy he cannot have dreamed of taking part in.

If he was what our farrier calls a 'khaki brain', it was in the pleasantest possible way. The war, and the Dorset Regiment, had been central to his life. I admired him for it, and would try to hide my smiles when he asked 'You remember Colonel this, or Major that…?', naming officers, his heroes, who were possibly already in their graves when I joined my regiment as a peace-time soldier in the centenary year of Balaclava. When I visited him in hospital Mrs Palmer was always beside his bed, as she had been behind the counter in their shop; they were a devoted couple. At his funeral a bugler sounded the calls, and the chapel was full of his old regimental comrades.

It was on this day, 25 October, in 1854 that the 13th Light Dragoons charged on the right of the first line of the Light Brigade. Through the previous night they had been 'kept at their horses' heads from 5p.m. to 7a.m. The night was bitterly cold, and Major Willet of the 17th Lancers died of exposure', I am quoting from Cecil Woodham Smith's *The Reason Why*, but later, 'the chilly misty morning turned into a day of extraordinary brilliance and clarity'.

After a notorious and tragic game of Chinese whispers, mistaking his orders, that gallant nutcase Lord Cardigan, 'the very incarnation of bravery' and 'steady as a church', took his place at the head of his command and gave the order, 'The Brigade will advance. Walk, march, trot!', and so they went, so many of them, to their deaths. After the charge the 13th could muster only two officers and eight mounted men.

And what of the horses that were killed? Woodham Smith tells us that as long as they felt the hand of their rider, and his weight upon their backs, even when wounded, troop horses were singularly free from fear; but, once deprived of their riders, they became crazed with panic. That is a phrase that wrings the heart but rings true, and throws some light on the mysteri-ous elusive bond uniting horse and human. For their part, 'troopers, who had become attached to their horses, refused to leave them behind, and wounded bleeding men staggered along, dragging with them wounded and bleeding beasts'.

Spare a thought today for the men and horses of the Light Brigade.

DECEMBER

'The bridle that your husband left for mending is ready, if you would like to take it' said the lady in the saddler's shop innocently to my wife, when she was in there Christmas shopping. Somehow I had not found exactly the right moment to confess that I had carelessly allowed Dandy to trample on his reins ('You are just not with it these days darling, always daydreaming, head up in the clouds somewhere – its ever since you started writing!'). It often seems impossible to keep a secret, least of all from one's nearest and dearest.

I have been luckier about the stock. Not often volunteering my services in the kitchen, the other evening I for once begged to be allowed to try to make soup out of a duck carcass that was heading for the dustbin. I put it to swim with an onion in the 'bottom aga' overnight. The coast being clear next day I set about boning it when, in an evil moment, my eye fell on the liquidiser.

My knowledge of this gadget was theoretical, based on observation only. I thought that I knew what to do, but was rather taken by surprise when it behaved as if I had struck oil, or struck duck rather. A palmtree of rich, beautiful smelling stock sprouted out of a hole in the lid of the wretched thing, covering me and large part of the kitchen with tiny, no doubt delicious, bits of bird and onion.

It was a nightmare. 'Do be careful not spill any' my wife had cautioned as she left. The words echoed in my head as I frantically tried to clean up what looked like *Grand Guignol*, in sepia. The job done, I found employment in the carpentry shed until supper time, when somewhat tentatively, antennae fully mounted, I reconnected with indoors.

Nothing was said until breakfast on the following day when: 'Did you spill the duck, darling?' 'Er... why do you ask?' 'I keep finding little bits of it' ... 'Well yes, I'm afraid, some did get spilled' I replied, diving into the newspaper, and that was that. Against all the odds I seem to have got away with 'quacker-gate': the stock went into a game pie.

My wife has a system of cabalistic writing, squiggles and hieroglyphs, with which she very sensibly keeps me in ignorance of the contents of the diary, telling me day by day, or earlier if I should need to know, what the duties of the hour might be. It is quite usual, for instance, for me to learn casually chatting with neighbours the delightful news that they are to dine with us, and when.

For my part, I am very happy to live in this way, and grateful to have life organised for me. But, thanks to e-mail, which my wife has not yet mastered, I now have my own means of subversive communication with 'the children', my own enigma code. It is invaluable at this time of year, when Christmas presents call for endless anxious consultation and total secrecy.

October took us on a rare, long-promised, visit to Dale in Pembrokeshire, the very tip of the nose of the pig (did you not as a child think of the map of Britain as a witch riding on a pig?). As lovely a spot as it is remote, it seems not to have changed at all in the years that we have known it.

The small bay, with its castle and wreath of hanging woods, gives eastward onto Milford Haven, the roads busy with shipping, distant, but always full of interest… and memories. The booming foghorns one early morning years ago had seemed to threaten a day's foxhunting with the 'South Pem': in fact we had a wonderful day. The beach you might think was strewn with semi-precious stones, so varied is the colour of the pebbles. The call of birds, and the quiet are bewitching – I love Dale, there can be nowhere quite like it.

We were staying with old friends, she a noted animal painter, and fell for a large poultry scene hanging in their kitchen. Would she copy it for my wife's Christmas present, I asked via the enigma machine when we got home? She did better, she sold it to me, and smuggled it down by carrier whilst my wife was away being a grandmother in London.

I had thought to hide it behind the hanging clothes in my wardrobe, but had lost the scale of it in my head, it seemed enormous when it came to hand. And anyway I had begun to think that the excitement of sitting on the secret for two whole months was more than I could cope with, so I hung it, for a 'welcome home' surprise. It was a great success, but I am not sure that I am really the best person to be offering advice on keeping Christmas presents secret.

⚜ 2002 ⚜

JANUARY

At a time when much of the country is still oppressed by an unnatural silence the familiar voices of the 'Vale of Little Dairies', as Thomas Hardy named the Blackmore Vale, are especially welcome. Perhaps the most evocative these days is that of the stockman calling to his beasts – 'Ho! Ho! Ho!' or 'Hai! Hai! Hai!', or whatever. Artless no doubt, but with a distinct aesthetic quality, it might come from several fields away on a quiet evening, perhaps as the sun is dropping behind the Dorset Heights when I am settling our own 'beasts' for the night, late out at grass, half fit. It is a scene that brings Thomas Gray to mind, the first verse of his *Elegy Written in a Country Churchyard* is a soundscape if ever there was one.

But the best time for tuning-in is a frosty morning, preferably on a Sunday, riding out into the still vale, with only the clip-clop of the horses' feet competing with the stirrings of a late-waking countryside. The poultry yard, cattle, a lone cow protesting ancient wrongs, church bells, distant of course, (I am not playing hooky, we have evensong one Sunday in four), the faithful robin, who never leaves off singing, the soothing ringdove's 'Too true, my dear, too true', the manic yaffle (green woodpecker) or a rattled pheasant, I mentally touch my hat to them.

On a weekday there might even be the sound of a train on the single-track bathers' line, from Yeovil down to Weymouth. It is five miles distant, and I rather like the sound: but an old map in my possession projects a quite different story. A pencilled line slap through our village, with a tunnel under the Heights at Dogbury, marks how the railway would have run if some had had their way.

Rarely, just a few times a year, I hear deer. Richard Prior tells us, in his magisterial book *The Roe Deer*, that they are given to humming, peeping, rasping, grunting, barking, crying and screaming. I can only vouch for the last three, and I hope never to hear a deer cry or scream again. The bark he says is 'rather like that of a collie dog', but I think it is like nothing else I know. 'Who are you? Go away?' it seems to say. Once identified – hoarse, feral, menacing – it is unmistakable.

AS EARLY as the first week in December, Bella and I heard a thrush tuning up, and then, a few days later, putting together the bits and pieces of his full song, from the heart of Great Wootton Wood, under Dungeon: 'Did you do it? Did you do it? I saw you! Etc.' Then, on the shortest day of the year, after taking her brother Dandy for a much needed gallop, sinking the shoulder of that same hill I heard a sound I could neither credit, nor yet possibly mistake: 'Prruk... Prruk... Prruk!' Surely it must be some distorted echo. But no, flying up towards us, and then perching in an oak, enormous, inky black, like an idly furled umbrella, undeniable, it was indeed a raven.

Ravens have nested for ever on the Heights three miles away, but I never thought to see one down here, on the floor of the vale: whatever else, 2001 must have been a successful breeding year for ravens. This one, first of all obligingly flew over us, displaying its wedge tail. Then, apparently quite unafraid, it alighted on a branch less than 20ft away, and I studied it for a quarter of an hour – until Dandy made clear that he had had quite enough bird-watching for one day.

The sexes are indistinguishable, unless you should witness the cock bird's party trick of flying upside-down, but I felt certain from its extrovert, clownish behaviour that this was a male. He danced around on the branch above us, bashed it with his massive bill sending moss flying, toyed with a twig, and went through a raucous vocal routine that I had never heard before, including quacking like a duck.

Sometime in the nineteenth century the local landowner, perhaps he who saw off the railway, planted Douglas firs in the middle of many of his woods. They poke up like chimney-sweeps' brushes now, those tall Americans, head and shoulders above their native neighbours: I wonder if the raven fancied one for a nest site, and if he will settle here? The earliest of nesters, they will start building in a week or so. But the sight of him, and the sound of his 'very distinctive, deep, far-carrying voice' was one of the happier memories in a wretched year – that and the cry of hounds running through our ground just before Christmas.

MARCH

'See me dance the polka!' Bella seems to be saying, as she stands up and boxes the air with her mailed feet, and 'See me twirling round!', as she spins and fires off both barrels from her rear turret in the general direction of her beloved brother, from whom to be parted for so little as ten seconds turns her into a tragic heroine – Isolde, Tosca and Dido all rolled into one. I cannot remember any more of the words of 'Dancing the Polka' , but it was a cabaret act that we used to perform in the nursery as children, and no doubt picked up below stairs.

Horseplay is indeed rough. However much you may love horses, you cannot relax your guard with them – Bella would accidentally kick my brains out, and not give the matter a second thought until her evening feed was late. Only yesterday she trod firmly on my foot, then as I cursed, and helplessly pummelled her with my fists, as though deliberately, she shifted all the weight of her body onto that one leg in taking a leisurely stride towards her manger, before at last releasing me. But her antics at the bottom of the paddock set me thinking about a pre-war Somerset childhood. We used to go to some local grand house once a week for dancing classes, when we were put through such invaluable routines as the Highland fling and the sailor's hornpipe.

R iding lessons were another matter entirely. Apart from the war years I had ridden since childhood, but shortly after I first joined my regiment, in the 1950s, I had the great good luck to be sent home from Germany to attend riding school at Windsor. There were some beginners on the course, and I dare say that the Riding Master, the legendary Tommy Thompson, thought that I was too big for my boots. He put me on a horse with a notorious buck called Acre, who obliged by tipping me off one hard frosty morning in the Great Park.

When the Surgeon Colonel, a formidable figure, was checking my injured back, perhaps wishing to assure himself that I was fully fit for the rigorous duties of a Household Cavalry ensign, he ordered me to bow. Not having done this since dancing class, I made the deep obeisance with which we had been taught to conclude the sailor's hornpipe, no doubt folding my arms fore and aft in the approved fashion. 'A royal bow, you heathen!' the great man bellowed. Drawing himself up to his, it seemed, 8ft in height, and ducking his head to show me how it should be done.

The reproof was kindly meant, but to a pea-green cavalry-of-the-line subaltern, a country doctor's son, who had not been at all in the way of meeting royalty, it stung. I don't really reckon much to dancing lessons for small boys; they don't seem to be a great help to one in later life.

Despite her high spirits, or perhaps because of them, Bella is a lovely ride. Like her brother she is bombproof in traffic, but I seriously wonder for how much longer it will be safe for horses to be ridden on our roads. Twice a week I take Dandy, whose purpose in life is more than purely ornamental, for a bit of hill work and a pipe-opener, leaving Bella lamenting in her box, 'Visi d'arte, visi d'amore... etc'. Once a week I give myself the treat of riding Bella on her own. But mostly the three of us go out together, she the led horse, and are confined to roads and tracks.

With rare exceptions, drivers are incredibly thoughtful and patient. For my part, I do my best to get off the road, so that they can go about their business without having to slow down, and always mime my thanks. Yesterday a familiar white van drove carefully by at a narrow place, the driver answering my salute with a brief wave of the one hand he was using to control the wheel. I am not sure if his smile was in answer to mine, or was intended for the person to whom he was speaking on the telephone.

APRIL

People who hunt seem to do so for any number of different reasons. When I first rode with our hounds, well over 50 years ago, what had me longing for hunting days was the joy of riding a really good pony, Pony Club fun, and no doubt various pairs of bright eyes. (Does anything set off a pretty face better than a velvet cap?) The huntsman was Will Maiden, whose son Bert whipped-in to him, and whose grandson Chris hunts the Berkeley hounds today. History does not relate how many generations that family goes back in hunting, but there can be no doubt why they hunt: it is in their blood.

It was only when I got to writing about the sport that I really started to take an interest in hounds. Whenever possible I used to spend time in kennels on the day before visiting a hunt, getting to know one or two individual hounds, whose fortunes I might follow on the next day.

Then, if I was very lucky, during the day the Field Master would give me the nod, and I would tag along with the Huntsman, go into covert with him, see at first hand how he conversed with his pack, and set about finding a fox. This way I learnt an admiration for huntsmen, their wisdom, skills and outdoor hardihood. As a class of people they strike me as being among the more worthwhile inhabitants of *Vanity Fair*.

The South Dorset, which has great tracts of forestry and heath, can go on hunting well into the spring, but I had my first day of the season with them only recently. We had started late of course, at Christmas, because of foot and mouth, but things had conspired against my getting out before. When I had given Dandy a minimal clip he promptly bruised a foot at exercise, and then twice trod off the padded shoe that the farrier had fitted to protect it.

But the day came. I had promised to attend a meet hosted by particular friends in the next village, and off we set – but not without hiccups. I had put my hat in the Aga, as I sometimes do, to soften it, and forgot it was there. It was very hot, though delightfully comfortable, when I went to look for it and remembered where it was. Perdita, who has not shown any inclination to follow the horses for some years now, decided for once to come with me: I had to turn back and place her in arrest.

A neighbour joined me as I cut across his field, and, as we jogged on the few miles to the meet the roads and countryside took on the bustle so well described in a book we had as children, called I think *Fox's Frolics*, and Dandy caught hunting fever.

I had decided in advance what I would do that morning, should the fates allow. I would see hounds find their fox, hope to view it, follow a little, jump a jump, and go home: the fates were kind, and we did exactly that. The field romped up from the meet above a hanging wood, Dandy more than a handful. They found and went away. We popped a post-and-rails on the Field Master's heels. Then I was as good as 'carted' over some lovely turf, pulled up, watched then out of sight and sound, and turned for home. Dandy was rather fed up, and so was I.

A few days later I set about dismantling the practice jumps in the paddock under a lowering sky, cutting up long-treasured whole trunks of elm and birch for the log pile. A heron flew over, not a common sight here, giving a raucous squawk every few beats of its enormous wings, looking and sounding more than ever like a pterodactyl. I watched it, expecting to see it glide down onto a farm pond on the edge of the village, out of sight, a mile away. But it suddenly turned on its side, somewhere over the pond, and dropped dramatically as if shot, just twisting to break its fall a couple of times. I hadn't known herons descended in this dramatic way.

The threatened rain came suddenly on. Perdita, who had been keeping an eye on me, whilst busy checking her bones in the midden, sprinted into the house. I heard her flap in the back door clap-to, but plodded on, the job had to be done.

Nerve of course comes into it, but I have found, in my 70th year, that getting myself and a horse ready for hunting, boxing to the meet, hunting, and then running the film backwards, is suddenly more fag than fun. I have at last given up regularly riding to hounds, from home – I think.

Driving down to a party in the south of the county that weekend I realised what I shall miss most. It is having the freedom of those Dorset hills.

MAY

I go to London sometimes as frequently as twice a year, but always, in spite of myself, return home with some happy memory. On the most recent visit, with time to spare, we went to the V&A to see an exhibition of tiaras, only to find that tiaras were 'off'; every available ticket had been sold. We writers are allowed hyperbole, so, crossing my fingers behind my back, I told the charming young lady at the desk that I had come up from Dorset especially to see the exhibition. It made no difference. Possibly she did not believe me, I was after all dressed for the Royal Opera House.

There is good loitering at the V&A, so we stayed on looking at this and that marvel until it closed, then took ourselves to Covent Garden. The Piazza is a grand place to be on a fine evening, quite my favourite part of London. I used to spend my lunch-hours there when serving a sentence in the Ministry of Defence. Redolent of the capital's past, particularly its literary history, it now has a charming present. Music and smiles everywhere, people bent on light-hearted pleasure.

At the centre of it all a string quartet was playing familiar classics in a wine bar in a sunken terrace. They were playing musically but clowning, delighting a responsive audience, clients of the bar sitting at small tables with a non-paying element leaning over a balustrade above.

La Sonnambula was a dream, and so was the restored Opera House; I am more than happy to have traded the crush bar for an air-conditioned auditorium. The opera's story is a simple one, an affianced village girl innocently sleepwalks into the squire's bedroom: nearly everyone lives happily ever after. The music is incomparable, and joyous. Bellini demanded extravagant athleticism of his singers, and Amina's final aria, with its ascending trills, is still beating in my head.

Next day, whilst my wife pursued her researches round the corner in Colefax and Fowler (there are over 70 sample paint pots currently in our house, swatches and patterns everywhere) I sat in the sun, with what in France passes for breakfast, at a café table in South Molton Street, watching the world go by. It was late breakfast time, and the world was bustling to work from tubes and buses in Oxford Street.

I never tire of studying such a scene, but soon my eye was caught by a group seated at a nearby table. A well-dressed, athletic looking man with a powerful face, balding, but with fair ringlets descending to his collar, was talking to three lesser, casually dressed men, two of them wearing brand-new, identical, and unconvincing black ankle-boots. Had they bought the boots especially for the occasion, why were they so clearly in thrall to 'ringlets', was he selling them something, or was he perhaps sending them out into the world on some mission? I simply longed to know.

Papers were shuffled, ballpoints plied, heads nodded, but only 'ringlets' spoke; his quiet impressive, educated, voice almost became audible to me as he warmed to whatever was his advocacy. I caught the odd word, but not enough to join the dots and make a picture. I hope that I have more sense than ever to attempt a novel, but I almost felt one starting in my head, written around the ambivalent aura of this stranger, his imagined past and future. But 'ringlets' just goes into the rag-bag of memory, along with two pairs of enigmatic ankle boots.

'*Pluie du matin n'arrêt pa le pelerin,*' said my companion, it was the Gallic equivalent of 'rain before seven, sun before eleven' I learnt. We were hastily changing vehicles at Over Stowey, it was pelting, the Quantocks quite invisible. 'I hope they have loaded the right horses' he added, as we pulled away from the livery yard for the long haul to Porlock, and up and on to Exford.

It was exactly a month ago. The offer of a sure-footed mare had tempted me out for the Devon & Somerset's last day. If the meet, in a steep cobbled farm-yard, evoked Lionel Edwards, or perhaps John Leech, such characters do you see hunting on the moor, the moor itself, its vast expanses peopled with groups of 'cavalry', was pure Orlando Norrie. There a distant solitary vedette, here a general with his staff, and there a squadron waiting orders.

A pilgrim's optimism vindicated, the sun at last came out. We had been on the move almost without rest, the going as heavy and as uncertain as only Exmoor knows. We lost hounds mid-afternoon, and turned two tired deserving horses' heads for Alderman's Barrow and the first leg of a long journey home.

JULY

All of us must have unconsidered treasures lying in the attic. I may have glanced at this particular document a dozen times over the years, as I rummaged through a box of papers looking for something else, thinking nothing of it. But evidently it snagged the memory, for about a year ago I went up purposely, fished it out, fetched it downstairs, and, for the first time, really focused on it.

A parchment, getting on for 2ft square, it had been folded twice, in quarters, was holed where the creases met, frayed and grubby. Now expertly cleaned and framed, it hangs under a tall window at the turn of the back stairs where it fronts me every morning as I come down first thing, and where I may give it an 'eyes-right' as I go up to bed. Compiled shortly after the Restoration, it is a royal family tree of the 28 kings and queens of England from William I to James II. A typical entry near the bottom reads 'Prince Rupert... now living 1678'.

Each generation – there are 21 of them – has listed across the sheet siblings and collaterals of the sovereign, each with a little box of detail about the size of a postage stamp, giving dates, achievements, and place of burial. All are minutely written in tiny italic script, in black ink, in an identical neat hand. It must have taken half a lifetime to complete, at the expense of goodness knows how many candles and goose quills – and just think of the research involved, there are more than 500 individual entries. It was evidently a labour of love, and of ingrained loyalty.

What a bore a lawn is. For all the work it demands you may get no more than a couple of evenings when you can entertain arriving dinner guests there; and perhaps twice the 'children' will sunbathe, say prettily how nice it is, and you feel rewarded. But really it is the birds that thank you – the lawn lies like a stage below my dressing-room window, with, on two sides, dense over-leaning bird-friendly shrubbery. It is a pleasure to witness their performances.

This year, we are being treated to a mystery play. Some enormous invisible birds have been using our lawn as a comfort station. They come and go, if you see what I mean, at dawn or in darkness every night, under our open bedroom window, in total silence, just leaving, by bird standards, two giant 'panda poos' – black and staring white. There is talk of an escaped eagle two villages away, and a not-so-distant neighbour has an AWOL peacock, but why don't we see the creature, or hear it?

The answer, which is no doubt already on the lips of many reading this, comes in today's post, from a guest who stayed the weekend with us and went on to shooting friends. Although all my bird books are too polite to mention it, partridges, it seems, are famed for their 'wondrous doings', which are even celebrated in verse. I cannot repeat the limerick here, but two of the triple rhyme endings are 'bird' and 'absurd'.

No such problem naming the nightingale that spent a few bliss-dispensing days in that same shrubbery before moving on to more suitable summer quarters. I heard it for the last time when I was walking Perdita, early, prior to setting out for a distant rendezvous with the Prince of Wales: I was writing something about his race-riding.

The interview took place at the end of a long, anxious day near Birdlip, high in Gloucestershire, where even in the second week of May many of the hedgerow trees still stood bare. When he had 'made much' of his polo ponies, using my first name, Prince Charles invited me to take one of two canvas chairs that had been set behind his car, and we got down to work.

Call me a hick, but I am not in the least used to royal circles. I felt that the country doctor's son had come a long way in life, thus to be greeted by the heir to the throne. 'Me too!' I sometimes mutter to myself as I come downstairs first thing in the morning now, my eye falling on that document so carefully drafted all those years ago by a long-forgotten royalist ancestor.

AUGUST

I found a wineglass sitting on a tussock at the bottom of a paddock a week or so ago: there is no possibility of it having got there by any human agency. It took a day or so for the penny to drop: a gate-crashing magpie must have lifted it from some shindig at the Village Hall, decided it had no use for it, or let it go in a fright. Catering stock, it is cheap moulded glass, but of a rather pleasing shape – what I think is called a schooner – I use it most evenings, toasting *la gazza ladra*.

The fragment of a smiling face that hangs, Cheshire cat-like, over a door in the oldest room in our house surfaced in the vegetable garden, once a cattle yard, some years ago – my younger brother found it. It also has a rational explanation. Visitors assume it is a death mask, but it is no such thing, plaster would never have survived underground. It is part of a Portland stone portrait bust from a memorial, no doubt discarded when the church was 'restored' in Victorian times, and whole north wall of the nave had to be rebuilt. 'You can dump that rubble in my yard' I can hear the rector say.

Can there be anything softer than the questing muzzle of a horse, when it thinks you might have a little something for it to eat about your person? But there is a hint of ivory in the velvet 'kisses' that Dandy and Bella plant on my bare forearms as I lead them in from the meadow of a morning – they are impatient for breakfast, so am I.

They seem to like the summer routine, and usually meet me at the gate. But the vet filed their teeth yesterday – essential every now and then to blunt the sharp edges their molars get from grinding corn. So this morning they briefly turn away at my approach, as if saying 'If its more dentistry, no thanks!'. But then thoughts of the manger won, and they came to me in their usual trusting way. We have been together all of their lives, and for quite a slice of mine: I do not like to think of a time when I shall not have their daily company.

I usually ride one or other, before returning them to grass. Today it is Dandy's turn – for an egg run. We ride through standing corn, follow-ing a tractor rut, meet a pair of roe-deer, get almost on top of them before they dance away, brother and sister probably, not an 'item'. Through Hay Wood, ford a tributary of the Caundle Brook, then rejoin the road, and, turning for home, pick up a dozen eggs from what must be the happiest flock of chickens in the world. They range over the site of a mansion, Middlemarsh Grange, that burned down a century and a half ago.

If I am lucky, someone will be there to help, and I will not need to dismount. Killing two birds with a single stone, I would then be able to pass on the latest news of our bus for the London March. The farmer, his wife, their lad and his girlfriend, and their immediate neighbours, are all booked onto our bus, which I organise by 'pony express'.

But today no one is there, and Dandy isn't as helpful as he might be over the eggs. He thinks only of helping himself, to whatever succulent foliage might be just out of range, as, at full stretch of his reins, I try to juggle the eggs into their boxes, get them into the bag that hangs from the saddle Ds, and put £1 into a shallow tobacco tin without spilling it. This done, we go rather gingerly home.

I don't normally meddle with the flower-beds, the vegetable garden is my 'part of ship'. But one needed a thorough dig – the wild sweet-pea that flourishes there has to be occasionally checked in its rampage. Digging two spits down I turned up a flint knife.

About the size and shape of the bowl of a dessert spoon, it fits with beguiling snugness between the thumb and two first fingers of my right hand, speaking its purpose. The 'blade', skilfully knapped in regular scallops, extends round one end and half of one side. It has some beautiful hues – I am bewitched by it, hardly like to let it from my sight.

On the day that I found the flint my computer, which I don't understand but am totally dependant on, failed. I wondered if my consternation matched that of the Stone-Age man who, I suppose, mislaid that precious tool on the forest floor a few thousand years ago, and whose hand last held it?

OCTOBER

'Did Jesus take this photograph?' piped my four-year-old step-grandson as, riffling through my mail, he lighted on a picture postcard. I was trying to smuggle him through his breakfast in the kitchen without rousing the remainder of the household: we are both early risers.

Doesn't the Bible teach us to expect wisdom from babes and sucklings – he was not that wide of the mark, the card had been sent me by my friend the late rector, as he and his wife sped towards Russia on their retirement holiday? Since he went on a fishing trip there a year or so ago, and the plight of the Siberian peasantry struck home with him, few of his sermons failed to mention Russia, and very good sermons they have been too.

'On the way to Moscow, visited St Hubert to venerate the Saint, and also visited the hunting museum...' my old friend's message read; absolutely typical of the man, his passion for hunting only rivalled by that for his calling. The picture that had caught Jasper's eye was of High Mass in the magnificent sixteenth-century *Basilique Grande Nef*, the apse crowded with scarlet and gold braid, and a-twinkle with the brass of *trompes de chasse*.

After Russia, our ex-rector is to rejoin that small part of his heart that has resided for some years now down west, in the Brendon Hills. How we shall miss him.

I wonder in how many kitchens across the country breakfast is taken in the company of a lurcher snoozing on a beanbag? Dear Perdita, grizzled now about her clever nose, and sometimes distressingly wobbly on her feet, is very much the old lady. What a corker she was when she first came to us, how she would fly a gate or cattle-grid; and what a martinet she was about the garden, no cat, fox, deer or rabbit would dream of trespassing on her manor, as they all freely do today.

It is all but 12 years now since she pitched up in the village, a gun-shy refugee from poachers or lampers on Dungeon Hill, half-grown, half-starved, verminous, wild with fright and insecurity.

A formidable huntress, her owner need never have gone hungry, but her hunting days are over now. When I tell her about the 'RABBIT!!' in the kitchen garden she just slopes off to her beanbag for a snooze – time was the very word electrified her: when we met a fox on the stable mound the other day she merely stared at it.

The accusing cobweb that enwrapped my face like cling-film as I passed through the door in the orchard wall to go to church the other Sunday had nothing to do with my old friend's recent retirement – more Sundays than not through the summer, when I should be on my knees I am on my way to some distant polo ground.

Now that polo has given place to hunting I shall go regularly to church again, or will try to anyway, it has been a more-or-less lifelong habit. But I shall only go when they use what I treasure as the birthright of every English-speaking child, *King James's Bible* and the *Book of Common Prayer*.

NOVEMBER

'Hounds? It must be Tuesday!' I said eight weeks ago, leaping out of bed. 'The horses will be excited' warned my wife – 'No more than I am' I replied, already halfway down the stairs.

Sure enough, there were skid marks by the gateway in the meadow. Dandy and Bella were at the far end of our five acres, chatting over a stile with the Hunt Secretary's horse in the road beyond. 'You woke me up – alright if I join you?' 'Of course' she said, and that is how the hunting season I had meant not to have began.

During my rushed breakfast Perdita sensed that something was afoot. She watched me, head cocked, trying to read in my eyes what the plan was, hoping she might be part of it. Having not volunteered to come 'riding' for ages, she came clattering out of her flap and tagged along as I set off down the drive, forcing me to lose time turning back to immure her. But hounds do not usually move far in autumn hunting, and I found them still busy in parish.

We had a great time. Dandy and I were sent on a VC mission, 'Stop them crossing the lane!' – there was valuable young stock beyond. Off we galloped, got to the lane just a hounds hit it. But they were easy to turn (they usually give not a bit of heed to me), and I sensed that they had over-run the line. I was right for once, and had the answer ready for the Huntsman: I was sure the fox had gone into the drain by the road, and it had.

My next day out with our hounds was shortly after the London March, the moon just a scrap past full. When I went to fetch the horses, Bella stood on the brink of a pool of her own shadow – there is surely nothing quite so Indian-inky dark as moonshade – and, as I put her halter on, her brother cantered round to join us from another division of the field. We left the field a comradely confiding trio, the whole world sleeping.

Bella has to be left in the stable when I take Dandy hunting. On her own in the field she would create mayhem, wake the whole neighbourhood, poach the ground horribly, possibly do herself an injury, probably cast a shoe, she is that sort of horse. But she is surprising quiet shut in her stable, so long as she believes no one is there to show off to. Whilst I am saddling Dandy, picking his feet out and so on, she continually turns the lights on and off, as though signalling to the *Luftwaffe*. She can reach the switch by stretching out over the chain in her doorway, loves to play with it, and I haven't the heart to shut the door on her until I must.

We had a longish hack, Dandy and I, in grey half light, the sun just beginning to outline the hump of Dungeon Hill. There was no traffic, just country noises, an owl hooting as it went off shift, cocks crowing, two out-of-season hand-reared lambs bleating for their bottle at a shepherd's door. I had been determined to make up for being late on my first outing, and we got to the appointed place before hounds.

There was no scent to speak of that morning on the edge of the dry chalk downland, but I heard the neighbouring pack speaking in the vale beyond Dungeon, and made a detour looking for them on the way home. No joy, but I seem to be well and truly bitten by the hunting bug again.

'Vot is 'vaste of r-r-rashuns'? asked our lovely Austrian gardener of my wife, when in my rough soldierly way I tried to express the opinion that a certain leggy shrub was not worth the space it took up in a flower border. I lost the argument to the ladies of the place of course, and slunk off into the vegetable garden, my proper sphere.

No one I hope would read this page in the hope of picking up gardening tips, but it occurs to me that I might share my wide experience of practices best avoided in the kitchen garden. Here are a couple of useful hints.

Do not net brassica against pigeons; it just gives the cabbage-white caterpillars a free run, gratefully protected from the small birds that usually eat them. I now have a platoon of skeletons in place of a really promising young crop of broccoli.

Secondly, if, in the autumn, you should chance to find a packet of leek seeds unaccountably lurking in the carpentry shed, save them for next spring. Do not try to plant them; they will come to nothing. That would truly be a waste of rations.

⚜ 2003 ⚜
JANUARY

Like it or not, by January my week centres on the stables. Nothing can be planned, nothing done, without first answering the question 'What about the horses?' – it is much the same as having a baby in the house.

I am not complaining. The pleasure and rewards of 'doing my own horses' never fade, it is just a wonder to me that I didn't know what I was missing through all the years that the army kindly provided me with a groom… which word reminds me that the one thing that I do not enjoy is the actual grooming.

In my view the Pony Club, and my big sister, made a ridiculous fuss about grooming, made a fetish of it almost. I am delighted to learn that our wonderful government, so prompt in stopping people doing things and trying us all up in bureaucratic knots, is apparently going to pass a law against 'grooming'. It is high time. Dandy and Bella, whose views on the subject entirely coincide with mine, will be delighted.

Clipping has no attractions for me either and I shamelessly buy my way out of that – the girl who does it for me actually says she enjoys it. As far as I am concerned, paying her is the best use of a £20 note that I know of. Dandy loathes it too, and behaves abominably. When we clipped him before Christmas the maximum dose for his weight of the sedative recommended by the vet left him bright and full of his usual bounce, entirely unsubdued, downright dangerous in fact.

We had to twitch him, which I hate doing, and which it takes him a day or so to forgive. On the morning after clipping he greeted me with a frown when I went to saddle him, and later nipped my bottom as I passed his box with the wheelbarrow, but we are friends again now. We don't clip Bella any more, she actually has to be put to sleep for the operation, which is immensely expensive. These days I just use her as a hack.

Dandy's first meet, after the season proper had begun, was on a day that opened with torrential rain. We sloshed our way down the Piddle Valley, through Puddletown, to the meet at Tolpuddle, where, taking the wrong route up to the unboxing field, I managed to stall the landrover. The trailer then started to slip sideways towards the deep cutting that held the track I should have taken. It was a bad moment, intensified by the handbrake not actually holding for a nightmare second.

I quickly unloaded Dandy, handed him to Will, our terrier-man, who like all experts in his profession, was immediately on hand when wanted. Then, when my rotten driving was just making things worse, swapped roles with him. Whilst I grazed Dandy, barely daring to watch, he somehow persuaded the vehicle to act on the greasy incline and inched it up, wheels spinning, onto the level of the meadow.

This was but one example of the knowingness and general superiority of the man on foot that those of us who ride to hounds are continually reminded of – it goes back, I guess, through infantry versus cavalry, to Saxon peasant versus Norman knight. You cannot win at one-upmanship if you are on a horse, it is a mistake to try, the only thing to do is to adopt a mien of meek apologetic cluelessness.

'I suppose you know that you have lost a shoe?' a foot-follower said to me on our next day out. Of course I didn't know – we had been nowhere near a road – and of course he knew I didn't know; it was all part of the same game, it ended my day and no doubt made his.

By definition, foot-followers come out solely to watch hounds. Not having the distraction of a horse to manage, or the hazards of getting across the country on another set of legs, often too they have binoculars, they usually know much better than the majority of us exactly what is going on. Few of us are too proud to ask.

Tacking Bella up is like struggling a naughty schoolchild into its Sunday best. She gapes shark-like at me when I put her saddle on, pretends she is going to fall down when I pick her feet out, and then greets the bit with a tight-clenched, letter-box, or No. 10 Downing Street, grin, refusing to open her teeth until she had been through the ritual of waving her head, me and the bridle around a couple of times, nearly breaking my arm.

On the day after Dandy lost his shoe, I was going through this fandango with her, preparatory to riding over to the poultry farm, when it was brought home to me that I was not the only one with eggs in mind. From somewhere down by the midden a song thrush started to belt out what must be the earliest, and most welcome, overture to spring.

MARCH

Twice recently I have found myself threatened with or by the law – it was a new experience. The first occasion was before Christmas. A group of us had gone to London for the second reading of the wretched hunting bill, and were to rally in Hyde Park, then march to Westminster to lobby MPs. For whatever reason, the police, and I am not ever, I hope, in a hurry to criticise them, gave us the run-around. When we at last got to the Embankment we were directed away from our objective, across Lambeth Bridge. It was very frustrating, especially as no reason was given to us.

Leaving the march, I nipped over the river and back across Westminster Bridge, before it was closed by mounted police, and so had a close view of the fun taking place in Parliament Square. If there was anything ugly going on I did not see it. The whole thing seemed hilarious, when suddenly, on orders from behind, the policeman standing a yard in front of me drew his baton, raised it, and did his best to look fierce at passive, bemused me. It was part of some rehearsed drill one supposes, but it looked farcical, self-parody, something straight off the stage.

I felt sorry for him, being put through such antics, but even more so for the police horses, which, at that moment trotted in briskly behind us from their heroics on the bridge. The one nearest to me, which could easily have knocked me down – we had no warning of their approach – a big, dark Irish Draught, looked scared and upset. I longed to comfort and to reassure it.

Our church stands virtually in the fields, aside from the village, but it is at the centre of a star of footpaths that, through the centuries, must have brought worshippers in from outlying settlements. One such crosses our meadow, on a beeline from a hamlet a mile away called Middlemarsh. It enters our ground, over a road, via a stile which has been there for as long as anyone can remember, beneath a great ash, once pollarded – undoubtedly a waymark, as such old pollards so often were.

By some unfortunate freak this path has been wrongly marked on the map, which shows it coming onto our land through the same hedge, but a few yards off. The error, little more than 40 paces, dwindles to nothing by the time the path leaves our field. Not a serious enough matter to bother busy people, you would have thought; but an officer from County Hall felt it worth driving out from Dorchester to spend the best part of a morning discussing it with me. I showed him how the path carried people direct from Middlemarsh to the church, and pointed out the old stile and the telltale pollard.

That he was not impressed became evident when I received a letter from him six weeks later saying that the map could not be argued with.

The definitive route is currently obstructed by fences and so cannot be walked. Anything that impedes the existing legal access is an obstruction and an offence under Section 137 of the Highways Act 1980. Work therefore needs to be undertaken to open up this route onto the definitive line or alternatively an application completed for a legal diversion.

I like to think that, as with the policeman in Parliament Square, my visitor, who had seemed a nice chap, and was evidently a countryman, has someone behind him issuing daft orders, because really this is crass bureaucratic bumbledom at its worst, a total waste of the council's time and taxpayer's money. If ever there was a non-problem that cried out to be left alone this was surely it. But no, under threat of prosecution they would have me bore a new hole in a stout thorn hedge, and put walkers and ramblers on the road for 40yds round a blind corner, rather than let them simply cross it, as they can do today and always have done.

I did weakly offer to go through the ridiculous rigmarole of applying for a 'diversion', provided that it cost nothing – but this he could not assure me. I will not spend good money, or waste further time, putting right someone else's trivial error.

So much for my second brush with authority: again the disproportionate threat, again the ludicrous self-parody.

I trust that you will believe me when I tell you that, on the very morning that I sat down with this article in my head, through the letter-box popped the winter issue of *Your Dorset*, 16 pages of self-congratulation from the county council, kicking off with the headline: 'We're simply the best', and, when you turn the page, explaining that, as usual, council tax is to go up again, by 'many times the rate of inflation', and implying that not a penny of our tax is wasted. I know better...

APRIL

The hunting season just coming to an end has not been a vintage one, at least I have not heard it described as such, but it has its special memories. The joint meet of four hunts that I attended on Exmoor in September, a prelude to the London March, was an occasion never to be forgotten. A day with Michael Hedley's Border hounds in the Cheviots will linger in my mind... until the next time. And I don't think I shall ever forget the tri-coloured horse with a gypsy name that I was lent when visiting the Axe Vale Harriers in January, he gave me a dream of a ride – I love coloured horses.

Then there was my day's coursing. The elegant greyhounds in their winter clothing looked so like thoroughbred racehorses, their handlers semi-giants (like Hagrid, to those in thrall of *Harry Potter*), one lost a grip on scale. The striking presence of those aristocratic stud-book dogs was perhaps what I most remember of the day; that and the heart-stopping bravura of the hares, by far the most of which, as always, eluded their pursuers.

Earlier, whilst we were waiting for the frost to lift, I had stood in the very room at Ibthorpe where Jane Austen slept when she visited her friends the Lloyds. I had looked through panes that had once refracted her gaze, stood, as it were looking over her shoulder, by the desk under the window where she wrote to her sister Cassandra, and noticed the crooked beam in the ceiling, as no doubt she did.

By late morning the sun had done its work, and we joined the Alresford Coursing Club, on Finkley Down, above Andover. Close by, two Roman roads make an almost exact St George's cross, itself bisected by the line of the much older Harrow (hard) Way. An ancient place, it is open farmland now, but one could picture it as much travelled and busily garrisoned two millennia ago. Perhaps the Romans coursed hares there: Arrian, Greek historian and Roman officer, gave us the earliest surviving literature of coursing and its rules, in the second century.

I had come with absolutely no idea of what the sport involved, supposing that a few kindred spirits with sight-hounds would meet on a hill and walk-up hares. Not a bit of it. A regiment of beaters, skilfully marshalled, and ranging very wide, funnelled hares towards the coursing ground, which was kept clear by a platoon of 'flankers'. A scarlet-coated slipper held a brace of dogs, one with a red and one a white knitted collar, and released them when a suitable hare appeared from behind him, and he had given it due law.

A mounted judge, also in scarlet, and evidently needing a sharp eye and a cool head, awarded points to each dog for its performance – three for the fastest dog, one for a turn, and half a point for a wrench (a turn of less than a right-angle). The course ended when the hare escaped into cover, or was killed, the judge then waved a coloured handkerchief to show which dog had won or removed his hat if there was no decision.

How to describe the fancy? There were 100 or so watchers, defying general description, all sorts, from toff to taxi-driver, and from far and wide, some had travelled the length of the country. And the sport? I had wanted to make up my own mind about this, perhaps the oldest of our country pursuits, one which politicians, and many who should know better, condemn sight unseen. I was riveted – by the athleticism of the greyhounds, and by the hares' resource, and can quite see why coursing has so many devoted followers and has survived so many centuries.

But perhaps the most enduring mental picture to outlive this hunting season will be that of my step-grandson, aged three, who flatters me with constant attendance when he visits us. He must have heard me leave the house for the early feed one hunting morning, because, when I was going downstairs for my own breakfast, he was squatting, a small doorstop, his bedroom door ajar, mousy quiet, finger on lip ('Must not wake Mama'), waiting to tag along.

Later, whilst he held the pin ready for me, I showed him how to make the knot in a hunting tie – trusting that I would not myself forget, it being the sort of automatic ritual that tends to deconstruct itself should you pause to think how it is done. He was staring up at me from knee-height, head on one side, quizzical, a slight smile on his face, watching intently.

Were we laying up a childhood memory? And, when Jasper reaches three score years and ten, will people still be knotting hunting ties on winter mornings, or coursing the wild hares on Hampshire's downs?

JUNE

'Good fences make for happy neighbours' is a saying that I learnt many years ago from our then gardener and odd job man. I have been reminded of its truth recently, thanks to the horses who are great leaners and stretchers, and are insatiably curious. Bella got into the way of robbing one neighbour's clothes-line, carrying off various embarrassing garments in triumph mid-field as trophies. Her brother Dandy, giraffe-like, would attempt to graze on another neighbour's hair as she took her ease in a favourite garden seat.

In neither case could you blame the horses, who were born in the village, are great pets, and were tempted into over-familiarity, usually by children, who love to feed them titbits. I do not complain. It pleases me that my neighbours cherish our horses, and I value every extra pair of friendly eyes taking an interest in their welfare.

Nothing can remit from a landowner's duty to fence his land securely against his stock. The problem is that, after the incredibly dry spring, it is impossible to get a fence post into the ground. Every sheep hurdle that we possess is now on temporary duty about the place, pending my doing a proper repair job when the ground is less impregnable.

'Leg-back, Stonylongs!' I called to the young farmer as Dandy and I clattered breathless into his yard. 'Thanks' he replied, stepping towards his landrover. It was a piece of luck finding him at home: albeit his wife would have done as well, though she has two small children at foot.

We had been setting off over my neighbour's meadow where some ewes, which had no business being in lamb were just coming to full term. Something had gone wrong with the chaperoning - 'The ram got amongst them, back along,' I had been told. All first-timers, some were presenting problems: Dandy and I did not need to get close to see that this particular ewe was in trouble.

Instead of diving into the world with two little feet and nose first, her lamb had just one leg out, plus a head with bulging eyes, his mother desperately straining. Two hours later, on our return journey, it was pleasure and a relief to see her on her feet cleaning her lamb off, conversing confidentially with it in the happy undertones that must be one of the loveliest of country sounds.

'La lotta continua!' I say to Bella these days as I approach her, bridle in hand – 'The struggle continues!' My wife and I are learning to speak Italian, every Tuesday for an hour, with a peripatetic tutor, round a neighbour's dining table. Old habits die hard. I scramble though my 'prep' shamelessly each week at the last possible moment: but I do practise my Italian on the horses. *Basta!* Is a word, an explosion almost, that I often have occasion for, and which they entirely understand – 'Enough!'

As we walk down the road Bella's metalled feet ask '*Quanto costa, quanto costa?*' (It's a good question, and the answer might shock those of you not familiar with modern stable economics. But the services of a good, patient, punctual, reliable farrier, who will shoe, hot, in your own yard, are beyond price.) Or if I am leading Bella '*Non mordere tuo fratello!*' is a rebuke often needed, usually followed by '*Non mordere il mio gnocchio!*', as she goes first to bite Dandy's neck and then my knee. If these are phrases of limited general use, they at least get me thinking about the next Tuesday's lesson.

A couple of times recently, in my rambles with Perdita around the parish picking up litter, we have found suspended in hedges, or stowed beneath them, plastic bags, ever so neatly tied up, containing dog dirt. This is the result of a bye-law or whatnot, which no doubt makes admirable sense in Bournemouth, but which has the daft effect here in rural north Dorset of preserving, if not for posterity, at least for several months, what would in the normal course of events have been washed harmlessly away by a few rain showers. I offer this as the best example I have come across to date of Dalrymple's Law, which states that 'Official activity usually has the opposite effect to that intended'.

JULY

Our strawberries have gone on very late this year, and have been rather tiresomely abundant. Jane Austen exactly describes the galloping ennui of picking strawberries, in *Emma*. Inside half a paragraph Mrs Elton gabbles, and no doubt gobbles, her way in an hilarious glissando from 'The best fruit in England - everybody's favourite... delightful to gather for one's self - the only way of really enjoying them...' to 'inferior to cherries - currants more refreshing... the stooping - glaring sun - tired to death - could bear it no longer - must go and sit in the shade'.

Mrs Elton was the vulgar bride imported from Bristol by the witless young vicar of 'Highbury', after Emma Woodhouse had turned him down. Coming to rural Surrey 'with superior knowledge of the world, to enliven and improve a country neighbourhood' – there's Austen irony for you, such fun

– Mrs Elton is surely the prototype of the worst sort of know-all 'incomer'.

I have been thinking of *Emma* and Mrs Elton more than usually recently. Not just because it is the novel that one most associates with summer – the strawberry-picking party at Donwell Abbey is followed in the next chapter by a picnic at Box Hill: the plot turns on these two outdoor summer scenes, – but because of a day recently spent at Chawton House.

Chawton, near Alton in Hampshire, was the village owned by Jane's brother, Edward, who had been adopted as heir by her wealthy Knight cousins, and who took their name. After his father died, he settled his mother and his two sisters in the cottage where Jane spent the last eight years of her life, from which all her novels finally went out for publication, and which was her home when she wrote the last four of them.

Edward Knight had other properties, and the 'Great House' was sometimes let, but we may be sure that Jane knew it and its grounds well – and we can be certain that they were at least in part the model for Donwell Abbey, Mansfield Park et al.

Now, Chawton House, which had almost fallen into ruin, has, over ten years, been miraculously restored, refurnished in period, and re-pictured. It is also the home of a priceless and unique library, repatriated in an act of quite extraordinary selfless generosity by its American owner, who has endowed the place as a centre for the study of Early English Women's Writing from 1600–1830. Unlike Jane Austen's cottage in the village, Chawton House is not intended as a tourist attraction, but one may go there, by appointment, to 'study the texts in context': I went there just to daydream.

Sandy Lerner, co-inventor of the Internet, has indeed enlivened and improved Chawton. Through her munificence, once again the New World has come to the rescue of the Old: how can we ever adequately thank her?

Modern Britain has little enough in common with Ancient Sparta. The risk-averse nanny state is no doubt a splendid hatchery for bureaucrats, just as it is a generous milch cow for lawyers, but it is scarcely the best seed-bed for the soldiers that it is so ardent to deploy here, there and everywhere. It was therefore reassuring, if no surprise, to find my old regiment much as I had left it, when they were so kind as to ask me to dine with them a short while ago.

The world's worst 'old comrade', I had barely been back in 30 years: but my regiment remembered me and within minutes of arrival I found myself visiting the stables. Stationed on an airfield in Norfolk, much of which county anyway, as Noel Coward has observed, lends itself to the game, they had lost no time setting themselves up for polo.

Although one squadron had only just returned from Bosnia, and the bulk of the regiment was warned for Iraq, and despite fire-fighting duties, they determined somehow to enter the Inter Regimental tournament. I followed their fortunes through the summer, watching what matches I was able to, until Goliath slew David in the finals. I felt very, very proud of them.

A great deal has changed since I was lucky enough to be given a turn commanding the 13th/18th Royal Hussars, now amalgamated with our old friends the 15th/19th as the Light Dragoons. What has certainly not changed is that the CO of the day, wherever and whenever, trustee of a wonderful tradition, has no more urgent task than that of attracting and keeping good young officers to command his troops of tanks or armoured cars, and to lead the men that crew them.

An enduring paradox of Army life, so difficult for a bureaucrat to grasp, is that, if the taxpayer is to get his money's worth, soldiering must be fun.

SEPTEMBER

Medieval theologians, so we learnt at school, got very worked up about exactly how many angels could dance on the head of a pin. The odd picture that this conjures up kept recurring to me as I was going through the rigmarole of filling in a passport application for my horse Dandy. How many newly appointed feather-bedded bureaucrats were balancing unseen on the pinnacle of this fatuous make-work scheme I wondered.

Dandy doesn't think much of it either. He showed a very proper distrust of the clip-board I carried into his stable, didn't know what to make of my reading glasses, and, when the stool that I stood on to examine the whorls under his mane suddenly collapsed into a heap of kindling, so did his waning confidence in my activities – he withdrew co-operation. No good telling him that I risked imprisonment or a £5,000 fine if I failed to file the application in time.

Whorls, by the way, are the little 'whirlpools' which you find here and there on a horse's coat where the hair isn't quite sure how it wants to lie –

if you have clipped your horse yourself you will know exactly where his whorls are, they demand close attention.

The placing of whorls is very individual, like a fingerprint, it is a useful aid to identification. Prodnose in Whitehall apparently needs to know precisely where all the whorls on the heads and necks of all the horses, mules and donkeys in the land are sited – such a shame he cannot be more gainfully employed.

'Your horse needs a passport...' a neighbour at a recent dinner table asked in astonishment when I broached this topic of the moment, '... where on earth is he going?' It was a good question. Apparently 'they' are worried that bits of Dandy might end up in a Belgian lunch-box, with all sorts of harmful veterinary drugs inside them – which shows how much 'they' know.

OUR village outing this year took us across the fields to the old coaching inn at Revels, long since a farmhouse, but, with its mellow brick façade and old outbuildings, one of the loveliest and most evocative local properties that I know. We travel behind tractors, well over 100 of us, mainly children, sitting on bales of straw on long trailers - it never rains; and we end up with a barbeque in the Village Hall.

Revels stands at the foot of the steep escarpment where the old turnpike climbed up onto Dorset's downland. Coachmen would pick up a 'cock-horse' at Revels, and tack it on in front of the team to help it up the hill, handing it over at the next inn, at Giant's Head.

Whilst we were being told about all of this a neighbour whispered in my ear that a centenarian had once told him that, in the last days of coaching they had a favourite cock-horse at Revels that used to take itself home, the coachman just turned it away at the top of the hill.

I find the picture of that horse, traces and reins carefully looped up, picking its way sagely home, irresistible. Sad if this fragment of oral history should be lost: I entrust it to this page.

OCTOBER

Once a chorister, always a chorister – or so it seems to be with me: I just love singing in church. Not the hymns so much, most of them are set too high, one just growls the melody line an octave down. And some of them have words that are embarrassingly bad, if you care about that sort of thing. But the words and music of the psalms and canticles are a constant joy.

Some time ago our then village organist, no doubt having heard me going wrong, gave me a battered copy of *The Cathedral Prayer Book*. Edited by Sir John Stainer, and dating evidently from the reign of our present Queen's father, it has all the chants, and, what is much more, the pointing. So when an unfamiliar psalm comes up you can sing it, as you ought, with robust confidence.

The flyleaf records that this particular prayer-book came to our church at Advent, in 1951. It has been painstakingly amended throughout to take account of the late King's death the following year. This has been done in heavy, black, rather Gothic script, with a broad nib, the letters, especially where the ink has run, not always entirely clear.

It was during our recent Harvest Festival service, the evening light not helping, and my mind perhaps wandering a bit, that I momentarily misread one of the rector's chanted versicles as 'O Lord, save the Quorn'. I will give place to no one in my devotion to the crown, but that seemed to me a very splendid prayer, to which many of us would say 'Amen'.

The telephone had rung on the previous evening, and sent me out at supper time to clean my boots. It was the new young Master of our hunt kindly telling me that he was bringing the hounds our way the following morning, just to check out a few places close by that he had not yet visited, before the season should open.

First thing next morning it was pitch dark, still and velvety warm outside, with that smell of burning leaves that is so typically autumnal. Bella was already waiting for me at the field gate, she must have heard me quit the house, but of her brother Dandy not a sign. There was nothing for it but to strike off diagonally across the five-acre meadow, hoping to stumble on him.

We were in luck: an inky hump, just that much darker than the surrounding gloom, struggled to its feet, and submitted to the head-collar, in return for the usual bribe. We came in, the three of us together, companionable, confiding, all else around asleep – one of the unforgettable moments of autumn hunting.

A tawny owl was calling as I rode up the hill out of the village, past the Manor House. I was counting its hoots, and, as if it were striking the hour, just on the seventh hoot, the hunt lorry ground up past us, parked, and dropped its ramp. Soon we were away off across the fields behind the hounds, just the huntsman, his whipper-in, my neighbour Billy and me. When I tell you that Billy was a radio operator in Lancaster bombers in the last war you will realise that the mounted field at the start of this un-advertised bye-day made up in years for what it lacked in numbers. A third joined us later in the morning.

There were no great excitements, no heroics called for. I was on and off Dandy many times, opening and shutting gates for the young Master. He drew a nearby wood, very thoroughly, and a length of the brook that marks our hunt boundary, his hounds finding several foxes, and accounting for a brace.

My friend Billy had a mishap, no harm done, but since he had a broken bridle and a strong, stroppy, young man's horse to manage, it was only neighbourly to see him safe on his way home. So ended my morning – I don't know how many days I shall get this season, but doubt I will enjoy any hunting more than I did during that almost private outing with our hounds on the morning of our Harvest Festival.

Next day I sang in a do-it-yourself *Messiah* in Sherborne Abbey. It was, as ever, utterly thrilling – especially as we did the Hallelujah chorus twice.

Home just in time to see the end of a TV programme on Beethoven, a question of dates drove me to the bookshelf. There, inside the flyleaf of a favourite reference book, was a letter from my old one-armed music master, the great Dr Douglas Fox, the most admirable man I ever knew. He wrote, wishing me well as I left Clifton, 'I hope that you will be able to keep up your piano [I never did] and perhaps the choral singing…' How's that for serendipity?

DECEMBER

Since losing my wristwatch somewhere, as I supposed in the bilges of the yacht *Quicksilver*, in the Mediterranean, a couple of summers back, I have managed very well without it: the sun and my tummy tell me the time quite accurately enough. The watch was later returned to me, and I keep it in the 'toy-box' beside my seat in the kitchen, strapping it on before riding out of a morning only if there is a funeral in the village, or the farrier is due.

However, I forgot to do this one recent morning. It was at the start of the hunting season, and Dandy needed some serious muscle-building work. We went onto Dungeon and stitched up and down its steep flanks, strictly at the walk and trot (cantering, which Dandy would have much preferred, makes the exercise less beneficial), gradually working round the hill.

The old turf, certainly never ploughed in recent times, bears all the signs of ancient cultivation. When the sun is at a low angle, and the grass is close-cropped, shallow terraces can be seen traversing the western side of the hill. But on the eastern side there are dramatic 'strip lynchets', giant steps in the hillside where more spacious level fields were built to catch the morning sun. Presumably this was done by the inhabitants of the Iron-Age fort which gives the hill its name. It was whilst I was urging Dandy up one of these near vertical inclines that I suddenly remembered my neighbour's funeral. We hustled home.

I thought that I had time in hand, but there were raven figures grouped in the entrance to our drive. 'It's not until eleven?' I asked. 'That's right!' came the reply. 'What time is it now?' 'Ten to!' Crikey!' I said, urging Dandy into a canter. John Gilpin-like we clattered up the drive, arriving in the stable yard just behind the hearse.

Even if you learn nothing else at Sandhurst, you learn how to change quickly and present yourself at some challengingly remote place fit for inspection. It was lucky for me that it was my friend our new rector, not Jack Lord (the legendary Academy Sergeant Major), who greeted me as I burst through our orchard gate into the graveyard, but I made it, just in time, breathless, tie askew, tumbling into a back pew.

I find that I have to keep myself well in hand at funerals. The rubric in the prayer-book reads, 'The Priest... meeting the Corpse at the entrance

of the Churchyard, and going before it... into the Church... shall say...'
The 'sentences' that follow – 'I am the resurrection and the life... I know
that my Redeemer livith...', and so on – on such an occasion, and in such
a place seem to me so striking, so sonorous and majestic, yet comforting,
that they are quite difficult to bear with a proper composure.

The other trial is if we close the service with Hymn 477, 'The day Thou
gavest, Lord, is ended...'. I don't know who John Ellerton (1826–1893)
was, I can glean no more than his dates from my various reference books,
but what wouldn't I give to have left for the use of posterity those simple,
lovely, timeless words?

D andy was curled like a codfish, fast asleep, at the far end of the
paddock when I emerged from my siesta. It was a Sunday afternoon
and we had hunted on Thursday and Saturday, each an occasion that I
did not care to miss: why must life always come in lumps? We were both
of us shattered. I have the excuse of old age, however Dandy, aged 12, is
in his prime, but I suppose we must allow that, out hunting, it is he that
bears the burden of the day.

We have had a blessed rebirth of mutual confidence, Dandy and I. The
reason is quite simple, I have at last got him in the right bit. (Skip this if it
bores you, it is quite short in the telling.) Brought up always to hunt in a
double bridle, I tried that, a Pelham, a gag-snaffle, and both sorts of martingale, he fought with them all, was almost impossible to stop, and had
started to be shy of jumping.

Out with the Blackmore and Sparkford Vale one early morning this
autumn, a friend remarked, 'He opens his mouth you know', and my guru
at a schooling session said 'Let's ditch that martingale, it's cramping him'.
He goes now as sweet as you please in a snaffle and drop noseband: after
12 years of tactless blundering, it seems that I have got myself another
perfect hunter.

JANUARY

'Owhat can ail thee, knight-at-arms, Alone and palely loitering?' is the opening couplet from a poem by Keats that I stumbled on as a schoolboy, have much off by heart, and which occasionally surfaces in the rag-bag of memory. A powerful evocation of bewitchment and desolation, it is pure nonsense of course, much like Pre-Raphaelite pictures – I am fond of them too – and it suits a winter landscape, where 'no birds sing'.

We learn in later verses that the knight had unwisely given a lift to a dodgy lady, set her on his 'pacing steed', and became forever entangled in a nightmare in which fellow victims tell him 'La belle Dame sans Merci' has him in thrall. I found myself repeating some of these lines in my head more than once at the turn of the year, as I took my morning rides.

Can you bear one last slither of cold turkey if I tell you a little bit about our never-to-be-forgotten Christmas? We had four infant grandchildren, average age a fraction over two, staying for the best part of a week, with one of the mothers recovering from pneumonia. Much of it passed in a haze, pleasurable but burdensome, a grandfather's role being not unlike that of a pet mule, valued, but not expected to understand, merely required to be ever on hand and to obey.

The happiest memory is of being sent to church in charge of Jasper, aged five, and Sophia, three, with at the late minute a pair of apparently indispensable inflated water-wings thrust into my hand to take with us: what the village can have made of them I don't know. It was a short carol service, the lessons read by children. My young charges behaved perfectly, and I thoroughly enjoyed it.

The trick was to get out of the house, I found. 'On the run again?' a neighbour taunted, as she met me with the horses. If you have forgiven the helping of cold turkey, perhaps you will forgive a pun: I was indeed taking a breather from the madhouse, from bedlam *sans merci*.

There cannot be many more satisfying forms of outdoor winter work than hedge laying. The great joy of it is that it forces its own gentle pace on you, will not be hurried, and is totally engrossing. You find yourself working on into the dark, drunk with it almost, hating to leave off, and oh so proud of the product of your labour, although my work would certainly win no prizes.

There is nothing difficult about cutting and laying a hedge to a passable standard; nor is it particularly physical, women do it equally as well as men. I picked up the basics as a boy, watching hedgers working, but last year attended a one-day course in the Blackdown Hills, which corrected a number of misconceptions and bad habits.

What is heavy labour however, and a bore, is continually dragging clear discarded material: ideally you need an assistant to do this for you, as you work. First there is the rubbish, bramble, ivy and dead wood as you clean the hedge, then the surplus sound growth – you will probably use only a minority of the uprights to lay as pleachers. Very soon an enormous stack of waste builds up.

It was at Christmas that Jasper turned a corner in our relationship. Properly warned about thorns and prickles, a small boy makes an admirable hedging apprentice. For the first time in his life he was truly helping me with outdoor work, not merely 'helping'.

If it is therapeutic, hedging is also dangerous. My gauntlets being too wet one afternoon, I foolishly wore light gardening gloves, and stabbed my wrist with a blackthorn, to the bone. Just such an injury as hunters all too often suffer in this vale country, it was painful and swollen. The veterinary cupboard duly provided the remedy; an Animalintex poultice drew the wound, soothing it like magic.

Jasper and I were laying the hedge that divides our orchard from the lane to the church. Not least of the pleasures of the work was receiving the comments and compliments of neighbours as they passed, on what is a much-used walk. 'My grandfather used to spend the whole winter hedging'. 'That hedge will have a proper bottom now – it's a pity more people don't make hedges like that' and 'Well done – congratulations. You've done it properly, not used any binder twine', were typical remarks.

It occurred to me that a hedge made in the old way strikes a chord with people; they like to see it. There are not many things you can do about your land that are universally approved, and bring blessings on your head.

MARCH

Close encounters, even with common birds, and brief sighting of rare ones, leave a deep impression I find. There is something almost magical about our so different lives casually touching: no wonder the ancients read portents in such happenings.

This winter, for a few seconds, through a window, I saw a goldcrest doing its mousy foraging up a garden wall: it was just a few feet from me. The nearest thing we have to humming birds, goldcrests are tiny creatures. I once held one in my hand, having lost itself amongst the wisteria it had moused its way through a bedroom window and was fluttering help-lessly against the pane. It was like a fairy's feather duster in my palm: I can never forget the feel of it, or the bright colour of its crown.

One day in January I passed a solitary swan swimming majestically on a flooded field in the vale – we don't often see swans round here. On the following morning, five miles away, it flew over my head whilst I was out riding, purposely heading, it seemed, in the direction of distant Abbotsbury: no doubt its ticket-of-leave had expired. Ridiculous, but I almost felt it was aware of me.

Then, the following month, driving into Sherborne, I saw what I assumed, from its wing-span, to be a heron. But, when it banked suddenly, it showed a deeply cleft tail – it could only be a kite; I know that they are returning to this country after an absence of a century or so, but I'd never seen one nearer to Dorset than the Chilterns.

I could neither believe nor doubt my eyes. On getting home I noted down the date and 'Kite/heron. Holnest??!!' against the chance of cross-checking the sighting quietly with an expert should the opportunity arise. It doesn't do to trumpet one's credulity.

Butterflies have been much in evidence too this winter, I mean the figurative sort. Before Christmas an old friend asked me to speak at his wife's memorial service: she was someone for whom my wife and I had a very special long-standing deep regard.

As ever, the overriding fear was of not carrying oneself with credit, of letting the side down. I was in dread of not measuring up to the occa-sion, the worst part of which is being obliged to put oneself forward, when all attention and concern are due elsewhere.

The service was in Castleton, the hamlet on the edge of Sherborne that adjoins the castle grounds. Driving in with my wife I felt as I used to 50 years ago when I rode very incompetently in point-to-points. But it seems I got away with it; anyway, people were very kind.

Then, just a week or so ago, we found ourselves making the identical journey, this time with a trailer and horse behind us, in my case with almost the same sinking feelings. I had allowed myself to be persuaded to write up the very grand local hunt, when they were to meet at Sherborne Castle.

I used to go with the Blackmore Vale, as it was then called, as a boy, when, before mechanical hedge-cutting, you could scramble over the banks on a pony; these days I feel more at home hunting on the downland, with our own less fashionable farmers' pack, where we jump mainly timber. 'You know your way around, you'll manage', the Master had said. But the truth is I don't enjoy jumping big blind hedges any more, especially out of deep vale clay, they scare me.

Again, I needn't have worried. The hunt looked after me; they appointed as my pilot for the day a man of standing, an ex-Master, who was privileged and trusted to go where he pleased: he kept me in countenance, and, what was more important, in touch with hounds. I had an absolutely blissful time, and, a large part of the charm of hunting, got into parts of my 'native heath' where I had not been in years.

I long ago discovered that, for me, the trick of writing up a hunt is to relax and enjoy the day, and then find out on the quiet afterwards exactly where we went and what actually happened. That evening, sitting round their kitchen table with two of the joint masters, husband and wife, with sundry experts on tap on the telephone, we put the story of the day together.

A question arose as to the number of foot-followers out. My hostess rang the relevant authority, her husband remarking inconsequently, 'He's a 'twitcher'; did you know?' 'Ask him if I really saw a kite over Holnest church last week' I sang out. The answer came back, 'Oh yes, we've got kites alright'.

APRIL

'How much for the Canaletto?' I asked the man with the earring. 'I assume it's not an original?' he shook his head gravely, naming his price. As usual I was not sure who was kidding whom – if you are born fiddle-faced, irony often misfires. I went home to look the familiar picture up, to think about buying it, and plan where it might possibly hang.

In fact it wasn't a Canaletto. I discovered it illustrated in an old catalogue. By Claude de Jonghe, it was *Old London Bridge*, painted, in 1650, almost half a century before the great Venetian master was born. What can the man with the earring have thought of my ignorance I wondered. As the day wore on, finding that I couldn't live without it, I went back paid the asking price, and carried my treasure away.

I have never given more than 50 pence for anything at Sherborne rubbish tip before, but a pound seemed a reasonable price for the de Jonghe. It was a coloured print bonded on thick, heavy board, 4ft long by 12in, and in good condition, even though it must have stood several days of rain. It looks very much at home hanging in the summer-house.

There is a shame-faced but quietly enjoyable camaraderie amongst us bargain hunters as we inspect the goods on offer at the tip, I go there as often as I can find an excuse to do so – which is pretty frequently. It is amazing what people throw away, how one person's rubbish can be another's treasure – and vice versa.

My best previous finds were a porter's trolley, and a full-sized agricultural trailer sheet, each bought for less than a pound. But what I find almost impossible to resist are other men's oddment boxes. Lifetime collections of screws, nails and so on, no doubt discarded 'when granddad died'. I have several of them now on my bench, and love rummaging in them: but there cannot be much doubt as to where they will eventually end up.

Almost exactly, to the week, 50 years after I myself passed out at Sandhurst my wife and I returned to see a niece, a young captain in the RAVC, on her Final Parade. She was one of 40 professionally qualified officers who had attended a short training course there. We felt very proud of her, and it was a simply lovely occasion. Jack Lord, the legendary Academy Sergeant Major, used to drill it into us that 'Sandhurst is the Home of the British Army'. It felt just like returning home, much changed of course, but so much reassuringly the same.

Two memories stand out. Meeting an old (in)subordinate, much valued and put upon many years ago, who greeted me with the words 'Good Lord! Are you still alive?' That, and the 24-year-old black charger Sunningdale ridden by the parade commander, so splendid in presence and so self-possessed, ears pricked, and plonking his great Irish feet down in time to the music as he marched off parade. Sunningdale has recently replaced Snooker, retired as the Adjutant's horse for truculence I learn: so there's a change, the Adjutant of Sandhurst rides a black horse, not a grey.

The older I get the soppier I seem to become about horses. They have, 'in spades', many of the more admirable human qualities, but so few of the nastier ones.

JUNE

'Going anywhere near Dorchester, Duffy?' 'Nope!' said our invaluable farrier's back as he bent over Dandy's near fore, dressing the foot prior to fitting a new shoe from the pair heating in his mobile forge. Then, as he fitted the near hind, 'Where are you going next then, Duffy?' 'Piddletrenthide', came the laconic reply.

It was only when he was finally rasping the off hind that he said with a smile 'Were you by any chance wanting a lift...?' He's very 'regimental' is Duffy, Sergeant Fox that was, and addresses me by my old rank, though neither of us is in any doubt as to who is top dog now.

The exchange ended with me, at the double, a halter in each hand, turning our horses away in the meadow, before bundling myself into the front of Duffy's van. He dropped me off on what we call the 'top road', well on the way to Dorchester, before himself dropping down into the Piddle Valley and his next client.

The road south from Sherborne to Dorchester divides three ways at the foot of the downland – two roads follow the Cerne and Piddle rivers, the third, much the oldest, takes the high ground between. In prehistory a spur off the Great Ridgeway, it fell into disuse as the valleys on either side were settled. Then it had a brief period in fashion as a turnpike (toll road) in coaching days, before degenerating to the farm track that the US Army surfaced with concrete slabs to carry D-Day traffic – imagine the scene 60 years ago. It is a busy highway again today.

But, apart from the old coaching inn at Giant's Head, now a farmhouse, there is barely a habitation on it. It is not a good road to be benighted or to break down on: one uses it as a convenience when going out of an evening in fair weather, but usually comes home another way.

I had a four mile walk ahead of me, with breathtaking views across the heart of Dorset, and to the distant coast. It is not a Roman road as some people think, but the turnpike surveyors straightened the ancient track – speed seemed all-important then, as it does now.

The traffic as I walked was merciless; and many drivers graceless when, so that they need not slacken pace, I flattened myself un-thanked into the hedge. But worse by far was the roadside litter. It breaks my heart to see it: to this desecrated ancient way, which I have known, ridden, studied, loved and respected since boyhood, I must now turn a sad blind eye.

By an extraordinary chance my wife and friend emerged from a side-road returning from a girlie luncheon party – had I been a few seconds earlier we would have missed. I scorned a lift, but it was a welcome opportunity to explain my absence from home, where, in my hurry not to keep Duffy waiting, I had failed to leave a note.

High-minded folk scorn coincidence, and I believe it is frowned on in polite circles to exclaim how small the world is, but I find coincidence a source of wonder and delight. Hoping that you do too, I shall tell you of one that I don't think even the most scientific and dried-up philosopher could explain away.

On a charity 'Fun Ride' organised by the hunt at the close of the season, Bella and I fell in with an old friend who, for some reason – I forget the cue, it can't have been the weather, it was cold and wet – told me of how she had been saved within hours of death from dehydration in the Australian desert, was not allowed to drink, but was immersed in water. The feeling of her skin 'drinking' was something that she said she could never forget: this was news to me, that you must not allow the seriously parched to quench their thirst.

Next day I went for a final outing with the staghounds. The weather had changed, the sun poured down, and the Quantock switchback country took its toll. On our way home, I and my mount and our vehicle found ourselves involved in rescuing the huntsman's second horse, which was collapsing, must not be allowed to 'go down', and must quickly be got to a plentiful supply of water.

Loaded and heroically held on its feet by main force throughout a nail-biting journey, it was got safe to the hunt kennels. When soused with bucket after bucket from head to tail, its legs turned back from rubber to bone and muscle: like magic, it was soon ready to trample us all to death in its extreme of gratitude.

As the poor creature was being man-handled out of the box the cry had gone up 'Don't let it drink!' – now there's a coincidence.

TAILPIECE

When I am expecting a visitor who needs to be directed up our front drive, and away from the stable yard, which is the natural arrival point of this back-to-front house, I fill in time weeding the gravel. It got a very thorough weeding one recent afternoon, whilst I was waiting for the vet – he seemed ages coming, but I never wanted to greet a visitor less.

Perdita was lying sunning herself on the front lawn: that had seemed the best place to say goodbye to her. It was soon over, and she was gone... who had given us such joy, companionship and devotion.

I won't go on about a painful subject that most readers must know too well. Suffice it to say that Perdie just turned up here, a puppy, a dozen years ago. As we were to learn she was desperately gun-shy: I have no doubt that she was a refugee from poachers lamping on Dungeon Hill. A stunningly graceful creature, gentleness itself, she was our dream dog, just exactly what we had wanted and were half looking for. As I wrote on this page at the time, it was as if our guardian angels had put their heads together: hers was a fairy-tale life.